IN THE LOOP

A Reference
Guide to
American
English Idioms

In the Loop:
A Reference Guide to American English Idioms

Published by the Office of English Language Programs
United States Department of State
Washington, DC 20037

First Edition 2010

Adapted from:
Something to Crow About by Shelley Vance Laflin;
ed. Anna Maria Malkoç, Frank Smolinski

Illustrated American Idioms by Dean Curry

Special thanks to Elizabeth Ball for copyediting
and proofreading this 2010 edition.

Office of English Language Programs
Bureau of Cultural and Educational Affairs
United States Department of State
Washington, DC 20037
englishprograms.state.gov

Contents

Introduction

Idiom: a group of words that means something different than the individual words it contains

As with any language, American English is full of idioms, especially when spoken. Idioms add color and texture to language by creating images that convey meanings beyond those of the individual words that make them up. Idioms are culturally bound, providing insight into the history, culture, and outlook of their users. This is because most idioms have developed over time from practices, beliefs, and other aspects of different cultures. As a culture changes, the words used to describe it also change: some idioms fall out of use and others develop to replace them. With idioms in particular, the beliefs or practices leading to their use may disappear while the idiom itself continues to be used. Idioms can be so overused that they become clichés; or they can become slang or jargon, expressions used mainly by specific groups or professions.

Idioms can be complimentary or insulting. They can express a wide range of emotions from excitement to depression, love to hate, heroism to cowardice, and anything in between. Idioms are also used to express a sense of time, place, or size. The range of uses for idioms is complex and widespread.

The complexity of idioms is what makes them so difficult for non-native speakers to learn. However, this complexity is also what can make idioms so interesting to study and learn; they are rarely boring. Learning about idioms, in this case those used in the United States, provides a way to learn not only the language, but a little about the people who use it.

In the Loop is a collection of common idioms updated and compiled from two previous books of idioms published by the Office of English Language Programs: *Illustrated American Idioms* by Dean Curry and *Something to Crow About* by Shelley Vance Laflin. *In the Loop* combines the popular aspects of the previous books, while also updating the content by including idioms that have come into use more recently and eliminating those that are rarely used. When available, background information is included about the origins of the idioms. Additionally, *In the Loop* includes categories of commonly used idioms and suggestions to the teacher to aid in developing classroom exercises for learning the meanings and uses of idioms. In essence, this book is intended to be both a teaching tool and a reference.

Organization of this Book. *In the Loop* is divided into three parts: Part 1, "Idioms and Definitions"; Part 2, "Selected Idioms by Category"; and Part 3, "Classroom Activities." The idioms are listed alphabetically in Part 1. Part 2 highlights some of the most commonly used idioms, grouped into categories. Part 3 contains classroom suggestions to help teachers plan appropriate exercises for their students. There is also a complete index at the back of the book listing page numbers for both main entries and cross-references for each idiom.

How to Locate an Idiom. In Part 1, "Idioms and Definitions," idioms are listed alphabetically by first word. The only first words not used to place the idioms in order are articles (*a, the, some*) and pronouns and possessives (*someone, one*). Instead, these are placed at the end of the idiom, separated by a comma.

How Each Entry is Arranged

idiom's main entry

definition of the idiom

sample sentences using the idiom

additional information about the idiom

cross-referenced idioms for comparison

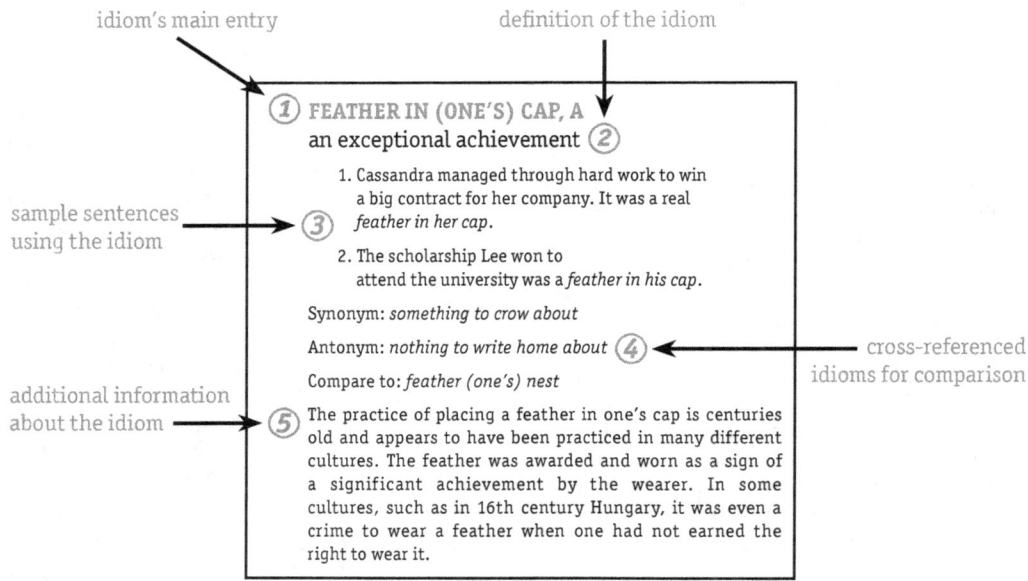

(1) FEATHER IN (ONE'S) CAP, A
an exceptional achievement **(2)**

> 1. Cassandra managed through hard work to win a big contract for her company. It was a real *feather in her cap.* **(3)**
>
> 2. The scholarship Lee won to attend the university was a *feather in his cap.*

Synonym: *something to crow about*

Antonym: *nothing to write home about* **(4)**

Compare to: *feather (one's) nest*

(5) The practice of placing a feather in one's cap is centuries old and appears to have been practiced in many different cultures. The feather was awarded and worn as a sign of a significant achievement by the wearer. In some cultures, such as in 16th century Hungary, it was even a crime to wear a feather when one had not earned the right to wear it.

The idiom (1) is given first, followed by its definition (2). Then, two or three example sentences (3) are provided to illustrate how the idiom is used. Occasionally, an idiom has more than one meaning. Where this occurs, each meaning for the idiom is numbered with corresponding numbers in the sample sentences. All entries include the idiom (1), definition (2), and sample sentences (3).

The final two elements—cross-referenced idioms (4) and additional information (5)—are included only where relevant or available. There are three types of cross-references used: *synonym, antonym,* and *compare to. Synonyms* are expressions that have the same meaning as the idiom. *Antonyms* are expressions that mean the opposite of the idiom. *Compare to* includes expressions that might be mistaken as similar to, or related to, the idiom. In the illustrated entry above, for example, *feather (one's) nest* has a completely different meaning than *feather in (one's) cap,* even though they both refer to a feather. The final section, additional information (5), includes notes such as the origins of the expression, restrictions on usage, or any additional information that might help a learner understand when and how a particular idiom is used.

Symbols Used in the Entries. Some idioms may have one or two alternate words that are used interchangeably without altering the meaning. One example of this is *in a fix/bind/jam.* In this idiom, *fix, bind,* or *jam* can be used without changing the idiom's meaning. In such cases the possible alternates are separated by a slash (/).

Some idioms require context-specific subjects or objects. In these cases *someone, something,* or *one* are placed in parenthesis within the idiom. *(Someone)* or *(something)* is used when the idiom's object is different than the subject. For example, in *beat (someone) to the punch, someone* is a different person than the subject as in *I beat him to the punch.* The pronoun *one* is used when the subject and object of the idiom is the same person, as in *ace up (one's) sleeve (He had an ace up his sleeve).*

Part 1
Idioms and Definitions

A

ACE IN THE HOLE
a hidden but effective means of winning a conflict

1. The other team thinks they can win this basketball game, but that's only because we haven't put our best player in yet. He's our *ace in the hole*.
2. It looked like the politician would lose the debate until he brought up his *ace in the hole,* an argument that nobody could refute.

The expression originates from some forms of the card game poker, in which players have both community cards and private ("hole") cards in their hands. To have an ace in one's private hand means that one can win the game without others suspecting ahead of time.

ACE UP (ONE'S) SLEEVE
to have an effective but hidden means to accomplish something

1. It looks like Joanne is going to lose, but I wouldn't be too sure. She may have an *ace up her sleeve.*
2. No matter how many times I think Paul might lose to me in a game of chess, he never does. He always has an *ace up his sleeve* and wins every game.

The expression originates from card games like poker, in which players might hide an extra ace up their sleeves to use in case they were losing the game and wanted to cheat.

ACHILLES' HEEL
a person's weakness or the vulnerable spot in his or her character

1. We've got to find his *Achilles' heel* if we hope to defeat him.
2. John appears to be a highly respected citizen, but I'm sure he has his *Achilles' heel.*

Achilles was a figure in Greek mythology who was invulnerable in battle except for his heel. It was the one weak spot on his body.

ACID TEST
the most crucial or important test of worth

1. Parents might be willing to buy this new toy for their children but the real *acid test* is whether or not the children themselves like it.
2. The *acid test* for laundry soap is not how well it cleans in hot water, but how well it cleans in cold water.

The expression originates from the use of nitric acid on gold to determine whether the gold was genuine.

ACROSS THE BOARD
equally for everyone, for everything, or in all cases

1. The boss made some people angry. He gave 5% pay raises *across the board* but some people thought they should have gotten more than others.
2. The car dealership was cutting prices *across the board*. Every car was on sale, not just a few.

ACTIONS SPEAK LOUDER THAN WORDS
the things that people do (actions) are more important than the things they say (words)

1. She's promised to be nicer to her sister from now on, but *actions speak louder than words.*
2. Every politician will claim that he or she cares about the problems of the average person, but *actions speak louder than words.*

This expression implies that we can learn about a person's true intentions by looking at what they do rather than what they say.

ALBATROSS AROUND (ONE'S) NECK
something or someone that is a burden and difficult to get rid of

1. That car costs you so much to repair. It has become an *albatross around your neck*. Why don't you get rid of it?
2. I hired my wife's brother to work in my business but he's worthless. He doesn't do anything. He really is an *albatross around my neck.*

Synonym: *millstone around (one's) neck*

An albatross is a large sea bird. The expression comes from the poem "The Rime of the Ancient Mariner" by Samuel T. Coleridge, in which a sailor shoots a helpful albatross with a crossbow, bringing bad luck on the crew of the ship. The other sailors hang the bird around the sailor's neck as punishment.

ALL KIDDING ASIDE
speaking seriously

1. That was a good joke, but *all kidding aside*, we have to get to work now.

2. What you're telling me sounds unbelievable. *All kidding aside*, are you serious?

ALL THUMBS
uncoordinated and awkward, especially with one's hands

1. I've tried to put this toy together according to the instructions, but I'm *all thumbs*. I can't seem to get the parts to fit.

2. Peter seems to be *all thumbs* today. He keeps dropping his tools.

ALL WET
wrong to the point of being silly or unbelievable

1. He's *all wet* if he thinks I'm going to believe his lies.

2. Don't listen to Maria. She doesn't know what she's talking about. She's *all wet*.

Compare to: *not know beans about (something); out to lunch; for the birds; talk through (one's) hat*

ALONG FOR THE RIDE, GO/COME
to be present for an activity without taking part in it

1. Janet's brothers went up into the mountains to do some fishing. Janet doesn't fish, but she *went along for the ride*.

2. I don't need to do any shopping, but perhaps I'll *come along for the ride* if that's okay with you.

The expression suggests that the ride itself is the extent of the person's participation in the activity, and that the person does not take part in the activity that is the purpose of the ride.

APPLE OF (ONE'S) EYE
a person or thing that is precious or loved above all else

1. Richard is so attached to his daughter that he would do anything for her. She's the *apple of his eye*.

2. The boy won't behave in school, but you can t convince his parents. He's the *apple of their eye*.

Centuries old, this expression stems from the ancient belief that the pupil of the eye was solid and shaped like an apple. The pupil was considered precious since one could not see without it.

ARMED TO THE TEETH
well-equipped with weapons

1. The police won't enter the bank where the thief is. He's *armed to the teeth*.

2. The invading soldiers were *armed to the teeth*. There was no way the defenders could hope to win.

The expression suggests having weapons (arms) from one's toes to one's teeth.

AS THE CROW FLIES
directly or in a straight line, without roads

1. The town is 25 miles from here *as the crow flies*, but it's over 40 miles by car.

2. *As the crow flies*, the airport isn't very far, but you can't get there directly. You have to drive around the mountains.

The expression is used to describe the distance between two points as an airplane or bird might fly, without taking into account the twists and turns in the road.

AT LOGGERHEADS
in strong disagreement, in a quarrel; at an impasse

1. They have been arguing all day about what to do. They really are *at loggerheads*.

2. John and Richard are *at loggerheads* about what would be a fair price for the car. John thinks Richard's price is far too low.

AT (ONE'S) WITS' END
at a loss about what to do next; in a state of frustration

1. When the woman looked around and couldn't find her little daughter, she looked up and down every aisle in the store until she was *at her wits' end*. She was almost hysterical when another customer in the store suggested that she notify the store's security officer.

2. We can t seem to persuade our son to stay in school. We have tried every argument we can think of, but nothing seems to help. We don't know what to do, and we're *at our wits' end*.

Synonyms: *at the end of (one's) rope*

Compare to: *keep (one's) wits about (oneself); use (one's) wits; scared out of (one's) wits*

The word *wits* means mental abilities.

AT THE DROP OF A HAT
on any pretext; without needing an excuse or reason

1. Those workmen look for any reason to stop working. They'll put down their tools *at the drop of a hat*.

2. Nancy really doesn't want to stay in her present job. She'll leave for another one *at the drop of a hat*.

no longer able to deal with a bad situation

1. I just don't know what to do with my son. He has misbehaved all day. I'm *at the end of my rope.*

2. We can't tolerate that dog anymore. We're going to give it away because we're *at the end of our rope.*

Synonyms: *at (one's) wits' end*

a hidden reason for wanting something or for not liking someone or something

1. Don't listen to Claudia when she tells you how bad that teacher is. She has had *an ax to grind* since he failed her last year.

2. Why do you keep telling me not to buy anything from that store? Do you really think they sell bad products, or do you have some kind of an *ax to grind?*

B

BACK TO SQUARE ONE, GO
return to the beginning

1. The editor didn t like the article I wrote for the newspaper. She told me to redo it, so I guess I'll have to *go back to square one.*

2. The builders constructed a building that didn't meet the city's requirements. Now they'll have to tear it down and begin building again. They're *back to square one.*

Synonyms: *start from scratch*

Compare to: *back to the drawing board*

Whereas *back to the drawing board* is used for the idea of re-planning or redesigning, *back to square one* can apply to starting any activity over. The expression originates from the idea of a game board on which square one is the square where the game begins.

BACK TO THE DRAWING BOARD, GO
return to the planning stage of a project

1. Our plan to raise money for a new swimming pool didn't work. Now we're *back to the drawing board* and trying to think of a better plan.

2. The idea of buying computers for the public schools through the lottery failed. The city leaders had to *go back to the drawing board* to think of another way to come up with the money.

Compare to: *back to square one*

The expression originates from the idea that plans and designs are developed on a drawing board.

BACK TO THE WALL, HAVE (ONE'S)
to be in a difficult or desperate situation

1. Gary lost his job over a month ago and he has spent all his savings paying his bills. Now he doesn't have any more money, and his *back is to the wall.*

2. My *back was to the wall.* It seemed like my only choices were to try to save the company with my personal savings or pull out and let the company go while I still had some money left.

Compare to: *in a bind; in a fix; in a jam; behind the eight ball*

BACKHANDED COMPLIMENT
a criticism that is phrased in such a way that it appears to be a compliment

1. Patricia said she can't wear fake gold jewelry the way I can because it turns her skin green, and I think she was giving me a *backhanded compliment.* She was really letting everyone know that she wears real gold jewelry while the jewelry I have on is fake.

2. Paul is not a very nice person. He is always giving people *backhanded compliments* that sound like he is being nice when he is really just insulting them.

Compare to: *damn with faint praise*

The term *backhanded* combines the meaning of *back* meaning insincere or malicious and *hand* meaning to give.

BACK-SEAT DRIVER
a person who gives driving orders when he/she is not the driver

1. Why must you tell me every time you see a red light ahead? I'm the one who is driving. Stop being a *back-seat driver.*

2. Andy's mother always made him nervous when he drove her to the store. She would tell him where to turn, how fast to drive, and where to park. She was a *back-seat driver.*

When cars were first developed in the 1920s, wealthy car owners would often ride in the back seats, telling their drivers where to go, where to turn, etc. Now such a practice by anyone is seen as intrusive and rude.

BAD BLOOD
negative or ill feelings

1. The young man and woman knew their parents would not approve of their marriage because there was *bad blood* between the families.

2. Those two brothers will never get along. There is too much *bad blood* between them.

BARK UP THE WRONG TREE
to misdirect one's efforts or argument

1. If Frank is trying to get a pay raise from the assistant manager, he's *barking up the wrong tree.* Only the manager can authorize a pay increase.

2. Janice is angry at me because she thinks I took her books, but she's *barking up the wrong tree.* I had nothing to do with it.

This expression stems from the 19th century American frontier practice of hunting raccoons using hunting dogs. When the raccoon attempted to escape up a tree, the dog was supposed to remain at the foot of the tree barking until the hunter arrived. However, if the dog went to the wrong tree, especially at night, or the raccoon jumped to the branches of another tree, the hunter would end up focusing on the wrong tree.

BATS IN (ONE'S) BELFRY, HAVE
harmlessly crazy or eccentric

1. You must have *bats in your belfry* if you think your parents will let you see that movie.

2. Don't listen to her. She doesn't know what she's talking about. She has *bats in her belfry.*

Synonym: *have a screw loose, out to lunch, off one's rocker*

A belfry is the tower of a church where the bell hangs, and is analogous to one's head. If a person has room for bats in his head, his head is full of space rather than brains.

BEAT A DEAD HORSE
to argue or pursue a point or topic without the possibility of success

1. They should give up trying to argue with the boss on that subject. They're *beating a dead horse*.

2. The boy kept asking for a motorcycle, but his mother told him he could not have one and she would not change her mind. She told him he was *beating a dead horse*.

Synonyms: *run (something) into the ground*

The expression is usually used to describe verbal communication.

BEAT A HASTY RETREAT
to run very fast in the opposite direction

1. The old man came out on the porch to chase away the small boys who were throwing rocks at his windows. When they saw him, they *beat a hasty retreat*.

2. The cat wandered into the neighbor's yard, but it *beat a hasty retreat* when it saw the dog.

Synonym: *make tracks*

BEAT ABOUT/AROUND THE BUSH
to speak or write evasively; to talk around an issue

1. Judy couldn't come right out and tell her fiancé that she no longer wanted to marry him. She had to *beat around the bush* until he understood.

2. If you disagree with my opinion, just tell me. Don't *beat around the bush*.

Antonym: *get to the point*

Synonyms: *stonewall; hem and haw*

The phrase originates from a hunting practice dating to the 15th century, in which hunters hired 'beaters' to drive small animals out of bushes where the hunters could more easily get to them. The beaters would lightly beat around the edges of the bushes to lure the animals out without completely frightening them away.

BEAT (SOMEONE) TO THE PUNCH
to do something before someone else does it

1. They decided to make an offer to buy the house, but when they did, they found that someone else had already bought it. Someone *beat them to the punch*.

2. Linda was going to invite him out to lunch but he *beat her to the punch*. He invited her before she had a chance to ask him.

BEAT THE BUSHES
to search exhaustively

1. We'll have to *beat the bushes* if we want to find another editor as good as Arthur was.

2. I've *beat the bushes* trying to find the right spare part for my old car, but I haven t found it yet.

Compare to: *leave no stone unturned*

BEHIND THE EIGHT BALL
in a difficult situation or position

1. Barbara's parents have told her to study medicine but she really wants to study law. How is she going to explain this to them? She's *behind the eight ball*.

2. My wife wants me to hire my brother-in-law to work in my company, but I don't want to because he's very lazy. I'm *behind the eight ball* on this one.

Synonyms: *back to the wall; in a bind/fix/jam; between the devil and the deep blue sea; between a rock and a hard place*

The expression comes from the game of billiards, or pool, in which the eight ball is always pocketed last. If one accidentally sinks the eight ball before the others, one automatically loses the game. Trying to hit another ball that is too close to the eight ball is seen as a risky situation.

BELOW THE BELT, HIT (SOMEONE)
to act unfairly

1. John told Robert about the job he was planning to apply for and Robert went out and got it himself! Robert doesn't play fair. He *hits below the belt*.

2. Mary introduced Sally to her boyfriend, Mike, and before she knew it, Sally and Mike were dating. That was *below the belt*.

The expression originates from the sport of boxing, in which it is against the rules to hit one's opponent below his or her belt.

BEND (SOMEONE'S) EAR
to talk to someone for a long time

1. I dread it every time that woman calls me on the telephone because she *bends my ear* about how her children don't appreciate her.

2. Don't mention politics to Bill. He loves talking about politics and he'll *bend your ear* about it for hours.

The expression usually has a negative connotation.

BESIDE (ONESELF)
distraught; very anxious and troubled

1. When the mother couldn't find her young son in the crowd, she was *beside herself* with worry.

2. I was *beside myself* when I realized the fire had destroyed my house.

BESIDE THE POINT
irrelevant

1. Your excuse for not giving me your homework on Monday is *beside the point*. It was due the Friday before.

2. Her argument that she needed a new dress for the dance was *beside the point*. We simply couldn't afford one.

3. The judge decided that the lawyer's argument was *beside the point*, and told the jury to disregard it.

This idiom stems from the idea of being separate from, or not part of, the main idea (the point).

BET (ONE'S) BOOTS

to be sure

1. Paula's never late. If she said she would be here at 9:00, you can *bet your boots* she will be.

2. I'll *bet my boots* that the salesman will try to get us to buy a more expensive car. They always do.

Synonym: *bet (one's) bottom dollar*

Whereas *bet one's bottom dollar* can be used in both the affirmative and negative, *bet one's boots* is used only in the affirmative.

BET (ONE'S) BOTTOM DOLLAR

to be sure

1. I know you think you're going to get that job, but don t *bet your bottom dollar* on it.

2. I'm sure they'll be married before the end of the year. I'd *bet my bottom dollar* on it.

Synonym: *bet (one's) boots*

Whereas *bet one's boots* is used only in the affirmative, *bet one's bottom dollar* can be used in both the affirmative and the negative.

BETWEEN A ROCK AND A HARD PLACE

facing two difficult outcomes for the same situation

1. Ralph found out that his brother cheated on an exam, and he knows he should tell the teacher, but he is hesitating because it's his brother. He's caught *between a rock and a hard place.*

2. The doctor told his patient that he had a very contagious disease and that it was important to tell his family. When the man refused, the doctor didn't know whether he should call his patient's family and tell them. He was *between a rock and a hard place.*

Synonym: *between the devil and the deep blue sea*

Compare to: *in a bind/fix/jam; over a barrel; behind the eight ball*

Between a rock and a hard place is more dramatic than *in a bind* and would be used when the problem of choice has no apparent or easy solution.

BETWEEN THE DEVIL AND THE DEEP BLUE SEA

facing two difficult outcomes for the same situation

1. I consider both Paul and Mitch to be friends of mine. Now they are mad at each other and each wants me to take his side against the other. No matter what I do I could lose one friend or both. I'm *between the devil and the deep blue sea.*

2. Dana's really *between the devil and the deep blue sea.* The boss wants her to lie about the financial state of the company. If she does, it would be unethical, but if she doesn't, the boss might find a way to fire her.

Synonym: *between a rock and a hard place*

BEYOND THE PALE

beyond or outside the limits of morally or socially acceptable behavior

1. That remark Jerry made wasn't simply in poor taste. It was *beyond the pale.*

2. Ron received an invitation to dinner and didn't have the decency to let his hosts know he wouldn't be able to attend. I think that kind of behavior is *beyond the pale.*

The word *pale* in this expression should not be confused with the adjective meaning "colorless." Here, *pale* means a region surrounded by a paling or fence and ruled by a governing body. In British history, the pale was the area in and around Dublin, Ireland, which was colonized and ruled by the English. Beyond the pale was anything outside this area. To the English, this was synonymous with being outside law and order, i.e. outside civilization.

BIG CHEESE

an important, powerful or influential person

1. You can tell he's the *big cheese* in this city because everyone listens to what he says – even the mayor.

2. She must really think she's a *big cheese*. She speaks to her co-workers as if they were her servants.

Synonyms: *bigwig; big shot; big wheel; head honcho*

BIG FISH IN A SMALL POND

a person who is considered important primarily because the place or setting is small

1. I accepted a teaching position in a small village overseas because I will have responsibilities that I wouldn't be able to get for years in a big city. I like the idea of being a *big fish in a small pond.*

2. Diane was a *big fish in a small pond* in her hometown, but when she moved to New York City, nobody knew who she was.

BIG SHOT

an important, powerful, or influential person

1. The company's *big shots* are getting free trips to Hawaii this year.

2. Now that you've been made a vice-president, you're really a *big shot*, aren't you?

Synonyms: *big wheel; bigwig; big cheese; head honcho, heavyweight*

The expression *big shot* is often used sarcastically or disparagingly.

BIG WHEEL

an important, powerful, or influential person

1. All the *big wheels* get the use of company cars and parking spaces right next to the door of the building.

2. Janet says she doesn t want to become a *big wheel* in the company because she doesn't want so much responsibility.

Synonyms: *bigwig; big shot; big cheese; head honcho, heavyweight*

BIGWIG

an important, powerful or influential person

1. Fred likes to think he's a *bigwig* but he really doesn't have much power outside his own department.

2. Did you see all the expensive cars in the parking lot outside? There must be a meeting of company *bigwigs* today.

Synonyms: *big wheel; big shot; big cheese; head honcho*

Compare to: *heavyweight*

The expression *bigwig* is usually applied to a person high up in a corporate structure.

BIRD'S-EYE VIEW

a broad view or overview of something or someplace

1. This outline will give you a *bird's-eye view* of my new book.

2. The flight attendant said if we sit on the right side of the airplane, we'd get a *bird's-eye view* of the Grand Canyon.

The expression suggests the view that a bird gets when it flies overhead.

BITE OFF MORE THAN (ONE) CAN CHEW

to take on more work or responsibility than one can accomplish

1. Sue plans to oversee the construction of her new house at the same time that she has taken on a lot of volunteer work at her son's school. I think she has *bitten off more than she can chew*.

2. They can't keep up with the number of classes they're taking at the university. They *bit off more than they can chew*.

BITE THE BULLET

to face a difficult or unpleasant situation

1. With our credit cards, we've been spending more money than we have. We're going to have to *bite the bullet* and figure out a way to pay for everything we've charged.

2. The doctor says you're going to have to change your life style unless you want to become very sick. It's time to *bite the bullet*, take a look at what you're doing to yourself, and change before it's too late.

Compare to: *face the music; grin and bear it; take the bull by the horns*

Whereas *face the music* focuses more on accepting responsibility for some misdeed, *bite the bullet* and *grin and bear it* focus more on preparing oneself to accept something painful or difficult. The expression originates from the practice where, before the days of anesthesia, a person undergoing an operation might have been told to bite down on a bullet to distract from the pain.

BITE THE DUST

to be destroyed or ruined beyond repair; slang for "to die"

1. The boss didn't like my proposal and he wants me to start over. Another good idea *bites the dust*.

2. I think this lamp just *bit the dust*. It broke and I know it's not worth fixing.

BITTER/HARD PILL TO SWALLOW

a difficult or unpleasant reality to deal with

1. John discovered the hard truth about responsibility. He didn't get his college application in on time and the school won't reconsider. It was a *hard pill to swallow*, but he had to learn the hard way.

2. Jill thought she was a good singer. When her brother told her she was tone-deaf, it was a *bitter pill to swallow*.

The expression suggests something that, like a pill, is unpleasant but cannot be avoided.

BLACK AND BLUE

discolored from a bruise; injured in a fight either physically or verbally

1. The girl fell out of the tree but didn't break any bones. She just had a *black and blue* knee.

2. James came out of the meeting *black and blue*, since he had made so many mistakes preparing the report without consulting his boss.

BLACK MARKET

a system of buying and selling illegal goods or goods at illegal prices or quantities

1. During the war each household was allotted a small amount of sugar and butter each month. If you wanted more, you had to buy it on the *black market*.

2. There is a growing *black market* for consumer goods that are difficult or impossible to find here.

BLACK OUT

to lose consciousness temporarily

1. After my operation, the doctor told me not to drive for a few months because I might *black out* and have an accident.

2. Tom was walking down the street in the hot sun. He became dizzy and then *blacked out*.

A *blackout* means a period of unconsciousness. The expression is also used when the electricity goes out in a city. As a noun, blackout is one word.

BLACK SHEEP
an outcast

1. I haven't seen my uncle since I was a child, because he isn't in contact with my parents. He's the *black sheep* of the family.

2. All the girls in that family except Mary grew up to become respected members of the community. She was the *black sheep* of the family.

The expression probably originates from the fact that most sheep are white and only the very different ones are black.

BLACK TIE
formal dress in which men wear black bow ties and dinner jackets or tuxedos and women wear formal, usually floor-length dresses

1. The dinner was *black-tie*, so all the men wore black bow ties and dinner jackets.

2. The film star's wedding was *black-tie*. It was a glamorous affair that I'll never forget.

The expression originates from the black bow tie that is part of men's formal dress.

BLOW (ONE'S) OWN HORN
to boast or brag

1. Keith lets everyone know that the boss is going to make him the new assistant manager. He likes to *blow his own horn*.

2. Ruth won't make many friends if she keeps *blowing her own horn* about her accomplishments.

Dating back to at least the 16th century, this phrase is a reference to the practice of blowing horns to announce the arrival of important officials such as kings. To *blow one's own horn* is to boast or claim a position of superiority over others.

BLOW (ONE'S) STACK
to become suddenly very angry

1. When Emily's father saw the damage she had done to the family car, he *blew his stack*.

2. I hope the boss doesn't *blow his stack* when he finds out I didn't finish this work on time.

Compare to: *raise Cain; fly off the handle; get (one's) dander up; blow off steam*

BLOW/RUN HOT AND COLD
to have mixed or inconsistent feelings about something

1. I don't understand Jack. One day he's really nice to me, and the next day he couldn't care less. He *blows hot and cold*.

2. Pam *blows hot and cold* about studying nursing. Sometimes she says she would enjoy it and sometimes she says it would be too much work.

BLOW OFF STEAM
to express one's anger, usually noisily and harmlessly, thereby relieving one's tension

1. Forgive me for yelling at you. I guess I just had to *blow off some steam*.

2. When my mother needs to *blow off steam,* she slams the cupboard doors.

Synonyms: *blow (one's) stack; fly off the handle*

The expression suggests the noise created when a steam boiler releases excess pressure.

BLUE
sad

1. Rachel seems pretty unhappy these days. I wonder why she's feeling *blue*.

2. Let's try to cheer up the children. They've been pretty *blue* since their pet dog died.

Synonyms: *down in the dumps; down in the mouth*

BLUE-BLOOD
a person (or animal) that is an aristocrat or from a noble family

1. The young man's parents did not want him to marry the woman he had chosen because they considered themselves *blue-bloods* and thought their son was too good for her.

2. The racehorses raised on my father's horse farm are *blue-bloods*—they come from a long line of Kentucky Derby winners.

BLUE LAW
a law which regulates personal behavior such as going to certain movies, dancing, or gambling

1. In the United States in 1920, a *blue law* was passed prohibiting the sale of alcoholic beverages. It was later repealed.

2. Some cities have *blue laws* that limit or prohibit such activities as dancing and gambling.

BLUE RIBBON
renowned (sentence 1); first prize (sentence 2)

1. The president assembled a *blue ribbon* panel of experts to study the problem.

2. Sally's science project won the *blue ribbon* because it was the best in the contest.

The expression originates from the blue ribbon that is often presented to the best entry in a contest.

BLUE-COLLAR WORKER

a person who earns a living doing manual labor, or generally uses his or her body rather than his or her mind to earn a living

1. Sam works on an assembly line mass-producing clock radios. He's a *blue-collar worker*.

2. People who work in factories doing heavy labor are usually *blue-collar workers*.

Antonym: *white-collar worker*

The expression originates from the color of the shirt generally worn by factory workers while on the job.

BOILING POINT

the point at which one loses one's temper

1. You've just about pushed me to the *boiling point*. In a minute I'm going to lose my temper.

2. Don't push the boss too hard about taking time off work. She hasn't had much patience this week and it wouldn't take much to reach her *boiling point*.

Compare to: *make (one's) blood boil*

The expression suggests heated water whose surface erupts with bubbles when it reaches a particular temperature.

BOMB

to fail completely

1. The playwright's new play closed on the first night. It *bombed*.

2. They thought they had hired an exciting speaker but instead he really *bombed*.

Compare to: *lay an egg*

Whereas *bomb* is usually applied to creative activities (e.g., a play, a book, a movie, an idea) that fail on a grand scale, *lay an egg* is usually applied to doing something that is socially embarrassing on a smaller scale.

BONE OF CONTENTION, A

a topic of dispute

1. The subject of politics is a *bone of contention* between Sandra and me—we never seem to agree.

2. John wants to send the children to a private school, and I think it's unnecessary. It's a *bone of contention* between us.

Compare to: *bone to pick, a*

The expression suggests a bone thrown between two dogs that would naturally fight over it.

BONE TO PICK, A

a dispute

1. I have a *bone to pick* with Anne. She told the boss I was looking for a new job and now he's angry at me.

2. You could tell by the angry look on their faces and the way they walked in looking for Jane that they had a *bone to pick* with her.

Compare to: *bone of contention*

BORN YESTERDAY

naive

1. Do you really think you can fool me? I'm not that dumb. I wasn't *born yesterday*, you know.

2. Philip is going to get hurt if he goes on trusting everyone the way he does. He never suspects that people make friends with him just because he is rich. He acts like he was *born yesterday*.

Compare to: *wet behind the ears*

The expression suggests that someone who was born yesterday has not learned to distrust or be suspicious of people and is therefore naive. *Wet behind the ears* suggests inexperience, while *born yesterday* suggests that the person is easily fooled.

BOTH FEET ON THE GROUND

(to be) realistic and practical

1. They're getting married very suddenly. They say they have *both feet on the ground* and that they have given it serious thought, but I have my doubts.

2. You're leaving school before you graduate? I don't think you know what you're doing. Are you sure you have *both feet on the ground*?

Synonym: *down-to-earth*

Antonym: *head in the clouds*

BOTTOM LINE, THE

the net result (sentence 1), or the simple and irrefutable truth (sentence 2)

1. You've told me about the down payment, the closing costs, the interest rate, and the price of the house. What's *the bottom line*? How much money am I actually going to have to spend on this house?

2. You and I can argue around and around on this issue, but *the bottom line* is that our children will have to go to college if they want to get well-paid jobs in the future.

Synonyms: *long and short of it, nitty-gritty*

The expression is often used to describe a monetary figure (sentence 1), but it also describes the basic, (supposedly) undeniable truth of an argument (sentence 2). The expression probably originates from the accounting practice of adding together the profits and subtracting the costs to arrive at a final figure under the bottom line on a spreadsheet or in a ledger or account book.

BOTTOM OF THE BARREL

the least able member of a group; the least desirable items from a collection

1. That's probably the worst idea I've ever heard! You've really reached *the bottom of the barrel*, haven t you?

2. I guess we can ask George to help. But in my opinion, we're scraping *the bottom of the barrel* if we have to turn to him.

Antonym: *cream of the crop*

This idiom is often used with the verbs "to reach" or "to scrape," as in the examples, and is used to express a negative opinion about a person or thing.

BOTTOMS UP!

a call to drink; to empty one's glass

1. We had better finish our drinks because the bar is closing. *Bottoms up!*

2. Young Timmy did not want to drink his medicine, but *bottoms up!* his mother insisted as she pressed the glass into his hands.

The expression suggests the idea that the bottom of one's glass will be up when one drinks. It is informal.

BOXED IN/BOX (SOMEONE) IN

restricted; to restrict someone

1. David feels *boxed in* because he is stuck in a dead-end job and he doesn t have any options.

2. Don't *box yourself in* by spending all your savings on the most expensive car and not having any money left in case of an emergency.

BRAINSTORM

to generate many ideas quickly

1. When faced with a complicated problem, it is often useful to *brainstorm* several possible solutions first before deciding on which strategy you will apply.

2. Before we began writing, our teacher asked us to *brainstorm* topics for our compositions.

Brainstorming is often a formal step in problem solving. The goal is to generate potential solutions without immediately evaluating them. Evaluation is carried out as a subsequent step. The word "brainstorm" is a verb, but its –ing form, *brainstorming*, is often used as a noun (as in the first sentence in this paragraph).

BREADWINNER

somebody that provides financially for his or her family

1. When Harold quit his job and went back to school, he and his wife needed to adjust to having one *breadwinner* instead of two.

2. When her family needed more money, Tara got a job after school to help out. She became a *breadwinner*.

BREAK THE ICE

to get things started, particularly by means of a social introduction or conversation

1. It didn't take long for the guests at the party to *break the ice*. By the time dinner was served, almost everyone was chatting with someone they had just met.

2. I'm afraid we haven't met. Let me *break the ice* by introducing myself. My name is John Taylor.

The expression suggests the idea of breaking through an icy surface to clear a path for ships.

BRING DOWN THE HOUSE

to be a great success

1. The comedian at the dinner show is wonderful. He *brings down the house* every night.

2. The music critic didn't like the new symphony being presented at the concert hall. In his newspaper review, he said it would never *bring down the house*.

The expression is almost exclusively used to describe theatrical or musical performances, but it could also be used for any event that would generate applause. It suggests that when an artistic performance is a great success, the audience applauds so noisily as to make the ceiling and walls of the theater collapse.

BRING HOME THE BACON

to bring money into the household to support a family

1. It's romantic to marry someone you love, but when you set up your household, you're going to have bills to pay. You should think about marrying someone who will help *bring home the bacon*.

2. Leo became ill and couldn't work anymore, so his wife went back to work. Now she's the one who *brings home the bacon*.

BRUSH-OFF, GET/GIVE (SOMEONE) THE

to be dismissed casually and almost cruelly

1. Sue accepted John's invitation to the dance, but when Wayne asked her to go, she *gave John the brush-off* and told him she didn't want to go with him.

2. The boss told me that he was busy right then and that I should come back later. I told him, "Don't *give me the brush-off*. I deserve an honest answer from you."

The expression suggests the idea of brushing a small piece of lint or dirt from one's clothing. It is usually used where one person is superior to (or thinks he is superior to) the other.

BUG

to bother, annoy, or irritate mildly

1. I told you I would have that report done by the end of the day, so stop *bugging* me about it.

2. The children *bugged* their mother about going to the movies until she lost her temper.

Compare to: *rub (someone) the wrong way; set (one's) teeth on edge; get (someone's) dander up; get (someone's) goat*

Whereas *get someone's dander up* means to irritate in earnest, *bug* means to annoy harmlessly or perhaps humorously. The expression suggests a bug flying around one's head.

BULL IN A CHINA SHOP

insensitive to delicate situations; to be so clumsy that one breaks things inadvertently

1. Tom was a bit of a *bull in a china shop* when he met his girlfriend's family, asking all the wrong kinds of questions about her relatives.
2. Larry can t take his son into the glassware store because he always manages to break things. He's like a *bull in a china shop*.

BUM STEER, GIVE SOMEONE A

bad advice or instructions

1. My stockbroker really gave me a *bum steer*. I bought a stock he recommended and it did nothing but go down.
2. Kim stopped at a gas station for directions to city hall. The mechanic told her how to get there, but he gave her a *bum steer* and she got lost again.

BURN (ONE'S) BRIDGES

to take a course of action that makes it impossible to go back

1. If you commit yourself to that course of action, you'll be *burning your bridges* and you won't be able to start over.
2. Anita decided she ought to leave herself the option of going back to school. She decided not to *burn all her bridges*.

BURN RUBBER

to accelerate with tires so quickly from a stopped position that the rubber tires make a loud squealing noise and leave a black mark on the street; slang expression meaning to hurry

1. The traffic light turned green. The car tires squealed as the driver pushed the gas pedal to the floor and *burned rubber*.
2. We're going to have to *burn rubber* if we hope to get to the wedding on time.

This expression is also used as slang for "hurry."

BURN THE CANDLE AT BOTH ENDS

to overwork oneself

1. Marie works all day and goes to school every evening, then she has to get up early in order to study. She's wearing herself out. She's *burning the candle at both ends*.
2. You really *burn the candle at both ends*. You've got to start taking it easy or you'll end up in the hospital.

The expression suggests that one is wasting one's resources or energy.

BURN THE MIDNIGHT OIL

to stay up late at night studying or working

1. If they expect to pass the test tomorrow, they'll have to open their books and begin *burning the midnight oil*.
2. The boss expects to see the new plans tomorrow. The only way I'm going to be able to finish them in time is to *burn the midnight oil* tonight.

The expression suggests burning the oil in an oil lamp for light in order to work in the dark.

BURNED OUT

lacking enthusiasm due to overexposure or too much of the same thing; completely used up; worn out

1. Scott just couldn t face another semester studying chemistry. He had taken so many chemistry classes that he was *burned out*.
2. Betty got *burned out* spending so much time volunteering at the hospital. She decided she needed a vacation.

The expression suggests a device like a light bulb that burns out (stops shining) when all of its energy is used up.

BURNING QUESTION

a question that deserves or demands discussion

1. I don't think there's any doubt that he loves her, but will he marry her? That's the *burning question*.
2. It's not a matter of which college he should apply to, since he can get into both of them. The *burning question* is, what should he study once he gets there?

BURY THE HATCHET

to end a dispute

1. This argument has gone on too long. Why don't we *bury the hatchet* once and for all?
2. I will always be sorry that my father and I fought before he died and I never got a chance to *bury the hatchet*.

Compare to: *clear the air*

The expression may originate from a Native American custom of burying a hatchet as a sign of agreeing to peace.

BUTT IN

to interfere (sentence 1) or literally to push one's way in between other people (sentence *2*)

1. This argument is between your sister and me, and it doesn't concern you. Don't *butt in*.
2. We've been waiting patiently in this long line, and that woman just *butted in* ahead of us. She should have gone to the end of the line to wait like the rest of us.

The expression suggests a ram butting with its horns.

BUTTER (SOMEONE) UP

to flatter someone, usually excessively, in order to gain a favor

1. My husband brought me candy and sent flowers, and now he's telling me how good my cooking is. I think he wants something and he's trying to *butter me up* so that I'll agree.

2. If you want the professor to do you a favor, just ask her. *Don't butter her up*.

This idiom is a reference to the act of 'covering' someone in praise or flattery, like covering a slice of bread with butter.

BUY (SOMETHING) FOR A SONG

to buy something very cheaply

1. Sue and Dennis found an antique painting in that shop, but the salesman didn't know its true value. It must be worth a small fortune, and they *bought it for a song*.

2. The man was desperate to get rid of his car, so I was able to *buy it for a song*.

The expression suggests that one can buy something by just singing a song.

BY HOOK OR BY CROOK

by one way or another; by any means possible

1. Margaret was determined to lose *25* pounds before summer *by hook or by crook*.

2. Bruce would be such an asset to this company, but there aren't any positions open right now. *By hook or by crook*, we'll have to get him a job in this office.

The expression connotes that rules or convention may be broken in order to achieve the goal.

BY THE BOOK, GO

operate according to the rules

1. The pilot might have carried out some preflight procedures more quickly, but because he was training a new pilot, he did everything *by the book* so the trainee would learn the procedures.

2. As a parent raising children, you can't always *go by the book* and follow the rules. Sometimes you have to use your intuition.

The expression probably originates from the idea that the procedure or accepted rules of an established game are set down in a book.

BY THE SEAT OF (ONE'S) PANTS, DO (SOMETHING)

to accomplish something by luck and instinct rather than skill

1. At the last minute, the boss was taken ill and Kate had to give the sales presentation. She was not sure of the best way to proceed, but she used the notes that the boss had prepared and followed her instincts. She managed the presentation *by the seat of her pants*.

2. The children had never cooked a whole meal or used the washing machine before. When their mother left in an emergency, they kept things going at the house *by the seat of their pants*.

Synonyms: *wing it; play it by ear*

BY THE SKIN OF (ONE'S) TEETH

by a very narrow margin

1. The thief leaped from one building to another to escape the police. He almost missed the second building, but he made it *by the skin of his teeth*.

2. Dan and Mark were swimming in the ocean and spotted a shark coming toward them. They swam to their boat and pulled themselves out of the water just in time. They made it out of the water *by the skin of their teeth*.

Synonym: *hair's breadth*

Compare to: *close shave*

The expression suggests that something is as narrow as the (nonexistent) skin on one's teeth.

BY WORD OF MOUTH

the informal, verbal passing of information from one person to another

1. Walter heard about it from one of the company's employees even though it had not been advertised in the newspaper. He got the information by *word of mouth*.

2. Jane and Sarah will be very hurt if they aren't invited to your party. You won't be able to keep it a secret. They are sure to hear about it by *word of mouth*.

C

CALL (SOMEONE) ON THE CARPET

to confront or hold someone responsible for some misdeed

1. The student tried to make the teacher think that his report was original, but the teacher knew it wasn't, and *called him on the carpet.*

2. I got *called on the carpet* for being late again.

Synonyms: *rake (someone) over the coals; chew (someone) out; read (someone) the riot act*

This phrase originates from the military, where it used to be that only senior officers had carpet in their offices. To be *called on the carpet* meant that a lower-ranking soldier was brought into the senior's office to be formally reprimanded for an offense.

CALL (SOMEONE'S) BLUFF

to challenge someone to carry out a threat or prove the truth of a statement

1. I told my parents that I had gotten passing grades in all my classes, but they didn't believe me. They *called my bluff* and asked to see my report card.

2. The bank robber threatened to shoot the bank guard, but the guard *called the robber's bluff* by walking up to him and taking away his gun.

This idiom is based on the literal meaning of this phrase as used in card games such as poker. A player who is bluffing may pretend to have a winning hand when in fact he or she does not. To call one's bluff in poker is to challenge one to show his or her cards.

CALL A SPADE A SPADE

to speak plainly or call something by its right name, even if it is unpleasant

1. Some people say Ben is generous with his money, but I *call a spade a spade.* He's not generous, he's foolish.

2. It's polite of you to refer to them as "lively" children, but let's *call a spade a spade.* They are actually very naughty.

Antonym: *beat about/around the bush*

The expression is usually used when something is described more favorably than it deserves. *Call a spade a spade* is a request for a more realistic description. The phrase dates back to ancient Greece, where the words for "spade," "boat," and "bowl" were very similar; the original translation my have been 'call a boat a boat.'

CALL THE SHOTS

to be in control or to give orders

1. In this classroom, the teacher is in control. The teacher *calls the shots,* not the students.

2. The lawyer tried to take control of the courtroom, but the judge reminded him that it is the judge who *calls the shots.*

This idiom stems from use in sports that involve aiming. For example, in darts, the thrower might call out the exact spot he/she expects to hit on the target. *Calling the shots* well shows the player to be in control of the outcome.

CAN OF WORMS, OPEN A

a situation that contains many unexpected and unwanted problems and consequences

1. The company's management thought their new policy would increase employee productivity, but instead it *opened a whole new can of worms.*

2. His situation is completely messed up; it's *a can of worms* that I'm happy not to have to deal with.

Synonym: *Pandora's box, open a*

CARRY A TORCH (FOR SOMEONE)

to be in love with someone, usually someone who does not love in return

1. Why don't you find a new boyfriend? Don t spend your life *carrying a torch for someone* who doesn t love you anymore.

2. Sara will never remarry. She will always *carry a torch* for Henry.

The expression suggests that love is a flame in the heart.

CARRY THE BALL

to take on work or responsibility in order to keep a project moving forward

1. We need more people to help get this work done on time. Are you going to sit there and do nothing or are you going to help *carry the ball?*

2. The people in the office were sorry to see Amira leave the company. She was such a dependable worker and you could always count on her to *carry the ball.*

CAST PEARLS BEFORE SWINE

to offer something to someone who cannot appreciate it

1, Buying our son an expensive car would be *casting pearls before swine.* He would be just as happy with an old used car.

2. Taking your young children to Europe would be like *casting pearls before swine*—they are too young to appreciate it.

The expression originates from the Biblical Sermon on the Mount, in which he says "Do not throw your pearls before swine, lest they trample them under foot."

CATCH (SOMEONE) RED-HANDED [GET CAUGHT RED-HANDED]

to catch someone in the act of committing some offense

1. The little girl's mother *caught her red-handed* trying to steal cookies from the cookie jar.
2. The two men dropped the stolen goods when they heard the police car sirens. They didn't want to *get caught red-handed*.

Dating from the 15th century, this idiom is a reference to the notion of killers being caught with the blood of their victims on their hands. The meaning later expanded to being caught in the act of any kind of wrongdoing.

CATCH (SOMEONE'S) EYE

to attract someone's visual attention

1. I was walking past some stores when a beautiful red dress in one of the windows *caught my eye*.
2. When the girls met their mother in front of the post office, they could see her walking towards them in the crowd, but couldn't *catch her eye*.

CATCH (SOMEONE'S) FANCY

to appeal to someone

1. Daniel arrived at the party not expecting to have a good time, but he met someone there who *caught his fancy* and spent the entire evening talking to her.
2. Before you decide that you don t want anything for your birthday, let's go to the jewelry store. You might see something there that *catches your fancy*.

Compare to: *tickle (someone's) fancy*

CHANGE HORSES IN MIDSTREAM

to change plans or leaders in the middle of some action or event

1. The president told the people that if they wanted the country to continue to move forward, they should reelect him. He said that to elect his opponent would be like *changing horses in midstream*.
2. The chairman of the board died suddenly before he could complete his plans for the company. The stockholders were forced to *change horses in midstream* and elect someone new.

The expression connotes that trying to change horses in the middle of a stream is not a wise thing to do—it would be better to wait until one is on land.

CHANGE OF HEART

a reversal of attitude

1. Karen told her boss that she planned to leave the company, but after the boss offered her a pay raise, she had *a change of heart* and agreed to stay.
2. The girl's parents said no at first, but then they had *a change of heart* and let her go to the dance.

The expression is usually applied to an emotional attitude.

CHARMED LIFE, LEAD A

to be lucky or avoid danger

1. That boy *leads a charmed life*. He always manages to avoid getting into trouble.
2. Monica *leads a charmed life*—she'll never have to work a day in her life.

CHECKERED PAST

a personal history that includes both successes and failures, or ethical and unethical behavior

1. Larry has quite *a checkered past*, but things are getting better. He has a new job and is saving for a new apartment.
2. The personnel director of the company refused to consider Mr. Dupont's application for employment because of his *checkered past*.

The expression originates from the alternating black and white (opposite colors) of a checker board. It is generally used in a negative sense, focusing more on failures and unethical behavior than on successes and ethical behavior.

CHEW (SOMEONE) OUT [GET CHEWED OUT]

to scold someone harshly

1. When Peggy came home three hours late, her parents were very angry. They *chewed her out* and told her she was restricted for two weeks.
2. The newspaper boy *got chewed out* by Mrs. James when he ran through her flower garden.

Compare to: *read (someone) the riot act; rake (someone) over the coals; call (someone) on the carpet; give (someone) a piece of (one's) mind*

CHEW (SOMETHING) OVER

to think slowly and carefully about something

1. I know the idea doesn't seem appealing at first, but why don't you *chew it over* for a few days before you decide?
2. Janice is not sure she is going on vacation in August. She's *chewing it over*.

The idiom probably originates from another expression, *chew the cud*, referring to the fact that a cow chews slowly and regurgitates its food to chew it a second time.

CHICKEN

scared; frightened

1. When the boy wouldn't jump from the high diving board into the pool below, his older brother called him *chicken*.
2. Are you too *chicken* to play a trick on the teacher?

Compare to: *chicken out*

CHICKEN OUT

to become too frightened to do something; to lose one's nerve

1. The girls wanted to ask the movie star for his autograph, but they got scared and *chickened out.*

2. You said you wanted to try parachuting, so we came up in this airplane. The door is open and it's time to jump. Don't *chicken out* now.

Synonyms: *cold feet*

Compare to: *chicken*

CHIP OFF THE OLD BLOCK, A

very much like one's parent(s)

1. The young man likes to do the same things his father does. He's *a chip off the old block.*

2. Now that Ralph has grown up, he and his father are as different as night and day. But when Ralph was younger, he was a *chip off the old block.*

Synonym: *spitting image*

The expression probably originates from the idea that a chip off a block of wood or stone, though smaller, has the same characteristics as the block itself. A *chip off the old block* usually refers to a likeness in character or personality.

CHIP ON (ONE'S) SHOULDER

a feeling of bitterness caused by a sense that one has been treated unfairly

1. I said good morning to Ed and he snapped back at me. He sure has a *chip on his shoulder* today.

2. Carl has *a chip on his shoulder* because he was passed over for promotion in favor of Maria, although he feels he was better qualified.

The sense of personal injustice is usually imagined. The expression originates from the custom of placing a chip on one's shoulder and daring another person to knock it off as a way of challenging someone to fight.

CLAM UP

to not say anything

1. The witness was ready to testify at the trial, but at the last minute she *clammed up* and wouldn't say a thing.

2. The boy's parents were sure he knew something about the theft at school, but when they asked him about it, he *clammed up.*

The expression suggests that one keeps one's mouth as tightly closed as a clamshell.

CLEAN SLATE [WIPE THE SLATE CLEAN]

a new beginning, usually achieved by removing any record of previous bad deeds (sentence 1) or debts (sentence 2)

1. The man had done some terrible things in the past, but he moved to a new town and changed his name. He was trying to make a new life with a *clean slate.*

2. If you pay me what you owe me, you'll have *wiped the slate clean.*

Synonym: *turn over a new leaf*

The expression originates from the idea of a slate, the forerunner to the blackboard, which can be wiped clean to allow for new writing.

CLEAN (SOMEONE) OUT

to take or steal everything someone has

1. The robbers broke into the bank at night and *cleaned the place out.*

2. We needed to go to the grocery store after the party. Our guests really *cleaned us out!*

This expression is sometimes used to describe stealing, but can also be used to describe legal situations where everything is taken.

CLEAR THE AIR

to resolve hidden resentment or uncover hidden thoughts

1. I must have done something to offend Louise—she's been so unfriendly to me. I told her I wanted to *clear the air*, but she just turned and walked away from me.

2. The boss called a meeting because there were lots of rumors flying around the office. He said he wanted to *clear the air.*

Synonym: *bury the hatchet*

The expression originates from the idea that when there is smoke or fog in the air, it is difficult to see.

CLIMB THE WALLS

to be uneasy or restless

1. Peter had been studying for more than ten hours, and he was beginning to have trouble concentrating on his books. He was starting to *climb the walls.*

2. That child's behavior is intolerable. If I'm around him for more than a few minutes, he has me *climbing the walls.*

Synonyms: *go bananas*

CLIMB/JUMP ON THE BANDWAGON

to join the crowd in following a popular position, cause, activity, or fashion

1. Susan was never one to follow the trends of the times just because everyone else did. You couldn't accuse her of *climbing on the bandwagon.*

2. The senator was a supporter of medical care for everyone in the country long before it became a popular cause. Now, however, everyone is *jumping on the bandwagon.*

The expression is often uncomplimentary. A person who is described as *climbing on the bandwagon* has not joined the crowd out of commitment, but out of peer pressure.

CLOSE SHAVE
a narrow escape

1. The driver was distracted for just a moment and nearly hit another car. He missed the other car, but it was a *close shave*.

2. The spy had a *close shave* when she was nearly caught in the military camp. She had to climb a tree just to stay hidden.

The expression probably originates from the idea that a man who shaves closely is narrowly escaping cutting his skin.

CLOSED-MINDED
unwilling to consider new ideas

1. I encourage you to try new things. Don't be so *closed-minded*!

2. Anyone who wants to make the world a better place will eventually have to contend with *closed-minded* people.

Antonym: *(keep an) open mind*

CLOWN AROUND
to act silly

1. The teacher asked the students to stop being silly. She told them to stop *clowning around*.

2. Jerry likes to *clown around* and is always playing practical jokes on everyone.

Compare to: *fool around; horse around; monkey around*

COCK-AND-BULL STORY
a story that is too unlikely to be believed

1. You want me to believe some *cock-and-bull story* that you're late getting home because you got lost and then ran out of gas?

2. The driver tried to explain his way out of getting a speeding ticket by inventing a *cock-and-bull* story.

Synonyms: *song and dance; snow job*

The expression originates from an English fable in which a cock and a bull had an unbelievable conversation.

COLD FEET
too scared to do something

1. Joel wanted to ask Mr. Lee for a pay raise, but when Joel saw him, he *got cold feet* and just said, "Good morning."

2. The soldier *got cold feet* when the pilot told him it was time to parachute out of the airplane.

Synonyms: *chicken out; have second thoughts*

COLD TURKEY
abruptly; not gradually

1. Harry decided to stop smoking cigarettes all at once. He decided to quit *cold turkey*.

2. Many doctors believe that if you want to give up using a drug, you can't do it gradually. You have to stop *cold turkey*.

This slang expression was originally used to describe a way of stopping the intake of addictive drugs, and is still used most often in reference to drugs, including cigarettes.

COME FULL CIRCLE
to return (figuratively) to a point where one has been before

1. Bruce practiced law in a small law firm, then taught law at a university, then gave up teaching and is practicing law again. He has *come full circle*.

2. We started with a small, two-bedroom house, but as the family grew, so did the size of the houses we moved into over the years. Now that the children are grown and have left home, we've *come full circle* and are moving back into a small house.

The expression suggests that in creating a full circle, one returns to the starting point.

COME HOME TO ROOST
to return to cause trouble

1. If you tell a lie, you may get caught up in it and find that it *comes home to roost*.

2. Dorothy is convinced that she is ill and dying because her unhealthy lifestyle has *come home to roost*.

The expression probably originates from the idea of a bird leaving and then returning to its roost, the perch on which a bird rests. It is usually used to refer to something bad happening to someone who has demonstrated some bad behavior in the past.

COME OFF IT!
a response to a statement that cannot be believed (sentence 1) or a behavior that must be stopped (sentence *2*)

1. You expect me to believe that you don't know how that dent in the car fender got there? Oh, *come off it!*

2. First you ask for juice and then change your mind and say you want milk. I get it for you, and now you beg for water. *Come off it!*

The expression is always used as an expletive in the command form. It is very informal and would normally only be used by parents with their children, or between equals.

COME OUT OF (ONE'S) SHELL
to stop being shy

1. Is that Tom dancing with all the girls? He used to be so shy and look at him now! He certainly has *come out of his shell*.

2. Patty has been sitting on the couch by herself since she arrived. Why don't you go over and start a conversation with her? See if you can get her to *come out of her shell*.

The expression suggests that a person who is shy or quiet is like a turtle that retreated into its shell.

COME OUT SMELLING LIKE A ROSE
to avoid blame that one deserves; to seem innocent

1. Larry should have gotten into trouble for what he did, but he was lucky and *came out smelling like a rose.*

2. Everyone in the government is accusing everyone else of wrongdoing and corruption. No one is going to come out of this affair *smelling like a rose.*

COOK (SOMEONE'S) GOOSE
to ruin someone's plans

1. Lynn knew that she was going to be in trouble for coming home late again. She wouldn't be able to talk her way out of it this time; *her goose was cooked.*

2. The students had sneaked into the classroom to see if they could find a copy of the exam, but now they could hear the teacher coming down the hall toward the room. *Their goose was cooked.*

The expression is used when someone is about to be punished.

COOK UP
to invent or plan

1. When Paul's friends planned his surprise party, they had to *cook up* a good excuse to get him to the restaurant without his suspecting a thing.

2. The prison inmates *cooked up* a scheme to break out of jail.

The expression connotes scheming, but is not necessarily negative (such as in sentence one).

COOL (ONE'S) HEELS
to wait

1. The assistant had a 3 o'clock appointment with his boss but the boss kept him *cooling his heels* in the outer office until well past *4:30.*

2. I'm sorry I'm late getting home. The professor had me *cooling my heels* in his office while he was on the telephone.

The expression connotes some degree of annoyance and would usually be used in informal situations.

CORNERED
trapped with no means of escape

1. The dogs chased the rabbit into the barn. It was *cornered* where it could not escape until the dogs' owner called them away.

2. When the police followed the thief into the back of the market, the thief tried to open the back door but found it locked. The police called out to the thief, "Come out now. There's no way to escape. We've got you *cornered.*"

Synonym: *back to the wall*

COST (SOMEONE) A MINT/ AN ARM AND A LEG
to cost a great deal of money

1. I really wanted that painting, but it *cost a mint,* so I decided not to buy it.

2. Sending my son to that college will *cost me an arm and a leg,* but it will be worth it.

Compare to: *pay through the nose*

The expression suggests that something costs all the money stored in a mint—a place where money is coined—or that something costs the same value as someone's arm and leg. Unlike *pay through the nose,* these two expressions are used for monetary payments only.

COUCH POTATO
a person who sits for long periods of time on the couch, usually eating snack foods and watching television

1. My boyfriend likes to sit around watching television all weekend. He's a *couch potato.*

2. Let's not sit around doing nothing. I don t want to become a *couch potato.*

The slang expression suggests that the person has acquired the shape of a potato because of lack of exercise and eating too much unhealthy food.

CREAM OF THE CROP
the best

1. The students in this math class are the best in the school. They are *the cream of the crop.*

2. That computer company never hires mediocre employees. It's such an outstanding company that they hire only *the cream of the crop.*

Synonym: *first-rate*

Antonym: *third-rate*

CROCODILE TEARS
false, exaggerated tears

1. I don't believe Tommy really hurt himself when he fell. I think he's crying *crocodile tears* just to get attention.

2. The little girl started to cry but you could tell she was watching everyone to see what kind of reaction she was getting. They were nothing but *crocodile tears.*

This expression comes from the ancient belief that crocodiles cry false tears to lure their prey.

CROSS (ONE'S) FINGERS
to hope for luck

1. I sure hope we haven't missed the plane. There isn't another one for a week. *Cross your fingers.*

2. We're hoping that the operation is a success. We *have our fingers crossed.*

CRY OVER SPILLED MILK

to be unhappy because of a past event that cannot be changed

1. There's no use worrying about a test you didn t pass. You can't make it up, so stop *crying over spilled milk.*

2. When Martin didn't get the job he wanted so badly, his father gave him good advice. He told him not to *cry over spilled milk* and that another, equally good job would come his way eventually.

Compare to: *eat (one's) heart out*

Whereas *cry over spilled milk* is to grieve over some event that has happened and cannot be changed, *eat one's heart out* is to grieve over an emotional situation that cannot be changed.

CRY/SAY UNCLE

to admit defeat

1. Larry and Nicholas were wrestling on the floor, and Larry pinned Nicholas down. When Nicholas was ready to admit defeat, he *cried uncle.*

2. Two children were fighting on the playground. The girl grabbed the boy by the hair. The girl told the boy that she wouldn't let him go until he *said uncle.* "Uncle, uncle!" cried the boy.

CRY WOLF

to raise a false alarm or exaggerate so often that one is no longer believed

1. Every Friday, that man comes in to the police station and says he thinks he has been robbed, but when we get to his house, there is never anything missing. I think he's just *crying wolf.* You can't believe him anymore.

2. Terry regularly lied to his mother, saying that his older brother hit him on the head. Terry did it so frequently that she stopped believing him and told him that one day he would be sorry that he had *cried wolf* so often.

The expression originates from one of Aesop's fables in which a young shepherd boy falsely alerts people that a wolf is attacking the sheep. At first, people respond to the boy's cries, but he cries "wolf" so many times just for fun that eventually they stop. When the wolf really does come and the boy cries "wolf," no one comes to his aid.

CUT AND DRIED

routine (sentence 1) or clear and unequivocal (sentence 2)

1. The boss said that there wouldn't be a problem with my getting a pay raise. I was long overdue for one, so the matter was *cut and dried.*

2. The case was *cut and dried.* It was clear to everyone that the man was guilty of the crime, and the best he could hope for was a short prison sentence.

CUT CORNERS

to do things poorly or incompletely in order to save money

1. It doesn't pay to *cut corners* by buying cheap tires for your car. You'll only have to buy new ones much sooner, and the cheap ones may cause you to have an accident.

2. Don't *cut any corners* when you write that report. Spend as much time as you need on it and do a good job. It will be important when the boss decides who gets the next promotion.

CUT OFF (ONE'S) NOSE TO SPITE (ONE'S) FACE

to injure oneself in the process of seeking revenge or attempting to punish someone

1. Sally was offended when she did not immediately receive an invitation to the party. When she got hers the next week, she refused to attend even though she really wanted to. She *cut off her nose to spite her face.*

2. When Philip looked at the first question on the test and knew he could not answer it, he became frustrated and refused to go on to the next question. He failed the test when he might have passed. *He cut off his nose to spite his face.*

CUT (SOMEONE) TO THE QUICK

to hurt or wound someone deeply

1. When Christina broke off their engagement, she hurt George's feelings terribly. She *cut him to the quick.*

2. I was very hurt when my son and daughter-in-law told me they wouldn't be spending Christmas with us this year. I was *cut to the quick.*

The expression suggests the idea of cutting live flesh (the *quick*).

CUT THE MUSTARD

to meet standards

1. The coach accepted 50 boys who wanted to play football. Before the regular season opened, however, he had to remove from the team those players who couldn t *cut the mustard.*

2. The captain of the ship was trying to assemble a sailing crew. He told all the men who applied that they would have to work long and hard hours, and that he would accept only those who could *cut the mustard.*

Synonyms: *make the grade; up to snuff*

Whereas *make the grade* and *up to snuff* can be used to describe both people and things, *cut the mustard* is only used with people.

D

DAMN (SOMEONE) WITH FAINT PRAISE
to criticize in such a way that one appears to be praising when in fact one is condemning or disapproving

1. Jeff told me that the diet I was trying was showing results, and he asked how much more weight I had to lose. He was really telling me that I'm still too fat. He was *damning me with faint praise*.

2. Alicia told me that she was never able to make her old shoes last more than a few years the way I could. She was really trying to point out that my shoes were old and that hers are not. She *damned me with faint praise*.

Compare to: *backhanded compliment*

In this idiom the word 'faint' means weak or feeble.

DARK HORSE
a competitor who is little-known by most people but who is expected to win by someone more knowledgeable

1. The voters know very little about Mr. Johnson, but he's a *dark horse* and I think he'll win the election.

2. At the racetrack, we placed our money on a horse most people had never seen before, but was expected to do well. He was a *dark horse* in the race.

The expression originates from horse racing jargon. It is often used to mean a surprise candidate in a political election.

DAWN ON (SOMEONE)
to realize something that was perhaps already apparent to others

1. I was surprised that there was so little traffic in the morning and that I was the first one to arrive at work. When no one else had shown up by 8:30, it finally *dawned on me* that it was a holiday.

2. A man came to Tom's house yesterday asking all sorts of questions about Tom's schedule. I asked Tom why it hadn't *dawned on him* that the man may have been a thief checking when Tom would be away from home.

Similar to: *see the light*

The expression suggests that the dawn reveals a situation. *See the light* means to understand, whereas *dawn on someone* suggests that one has been blind or slow to understand.

DAYS ARE NUMBERED, (SOMEONE'S/ SOMETHING'S)
there is only a short time before something ends

1. Judy always comes to work late, and I think the boss is going to fire her soon. Her *days are numbered*.

2. Your old car's *days are numbered*. It's only a matter of time before you have to get a new one.

The expression suggests that the number of days associated with a situation is not indefinite. It is often used about someone facing death or dismissal.

DEAD TO THE WORLD
fast asleep

1. Crystal tried to wake her sons to get them on their way to school, but they had stayed out until well past midnight and now they were *dead to the world*. Nothing could rouse them.

2. I was barely aware that my telephone was ringing in the middle of the night because I was *dead to the world*. I couldn t drag myself out of bed in time to answer it.

DEAL (SOMEONE) IN/OUT
to include someone in something, especially a card game

1. Mary thought their business venture was promising, but she didn't have a lot of money, so she told them to *deal her out*.

2. If you'll excuse me for a moment; I'm going to make a phone call. But I want to play this round of cards, so you can *deal me in*.

The expression originates from the idea of being included or excluded from a hand of cards in a card game like poker, and is still in reference to card games. It is also used figuratively in business ventures and other group activities.

DIAMOND IN THE ROUGH
an unpolished or unsophisticated person that has potential

1. Liz must have seen that Tim was a *diamond in the rough*, because she asked him out, and now they're getting married.

2. The boss always thought Sarah had little potential for advancement in the company, but he realized she was a *diamond in the rough* when she contributed some very useful ideas at the staff meeting.

The expression suggests an uncut diamond, which is unattractive to the eye but which has the potential of becoming a beautiful stone when properly cut and polished.

DIVIDE THE SPOILS

to give portions of the goods captured during a war to the winners of the war

1. Several centuries ago, it was common practice for invading armies to *divide the spoils* after they had won a battle. Whatever goods they had captured, such as money or livestock, would be divided among themselves to keep.

2. The boys from two rival camps decided to compete for a gallon of ice cream. The winning team would get to *divide the spoils* and the losing team would get nothing.

The expression is used literally in the context of war, but it can also be used figuratively, as in sentence 2.

DO AN ABOUT-FACE

to change one's behavior or mind abruptly and (often) apparently without reason

1. Yesterday, the boss said none of us could take our vacations in June. Then this morning, he *did an about-face* and said we could.

2. At first Ron's parents wouldn t let him have a car, but when they realized how much they would have to drive him around, they *did an about-face*.

The expression originates from the military command "About face!" which instructs a soldier to turn in the opposite direction.

DO OR DIE

to act out of necessity, even if the outcome is unpleasant (sentences 1 and 2) or to try one's hardest despite the likelihood of failure (sentence 3)

1. We decided the time had come to make a decision and act on it. As Harvey said to me, "It's *do or die*."

2. When the time came to mount an attack on the enemy, the captain said, "Men, the time is now. We *do or die*."

3. The boys tried their hardest to succeed. They had a real *do-or-die* attitude.

The expression can function as a noun phrase (sentence 1), a verb (sentence 2), or an adjective (sentence 3). When used as a verb, the expression is never conjugated (i.e., never "does or dies"), and thus is only used with I, we, and they.

DOG DAYS (OF SUMMER)

very hot days

1. Summer in the southern United States is uncomfortably hot and humid. In July and August, we suffer through the *dog days*.

2. I can't stand the *dog days* of summer. Next year I'm going to buy an air conditioner!

The expression has an astronomical source. It is the time in July and August when, in the northern hemisphere, the Dog Star, Sirius, rises in conjunction with the sun. In ancient times it was believed that it was the combined heat of Sirius and the sun that caused the hot weather.

DOG-EARED

well-worn

1. The pages of this library book are really *dog-eared*. A lot of people must have borrowed it and read it.

2. I've put the report in a plastic folder so the pages don't get *dog-eared*.

The expression suggests the idea of a dog's ears, which are pliable and limp, just as the page corners of a book become after extensive fingering and frequent turning.

DOG-EAT-DOG

ruthless, competitive, and fast-paced

1. Ed decided to quit his job in business because everyone seemed so dishonest, trying to get his job and steal his clients. It was a *dog-eat-dog* world.

2. John moved away from New York City to a small town in the Midwest because life in the big city was *dog-eat-dog*.

The expression suggests the idea of animals that are so desperate that they eat their own kind.

DO (SOMEONE) A GOOD TURN

to do someone a favor without having been asked and without expecting a favor in return

1. I contribute to a charity because, when I had very little money and no job, someone once *did me a good turn* and now I want to repay the favor by doing the same for someone else.

2. Sally is very loyal to her company because they had faith in her and *did her a good turn*. They gave her a job when no one else would hire her.

DOT THE I'S AND CROSS THE T'S

to be very careful and attentive to detail

1. We have to make this written proposal the best one they receive. We have to make sure we *dot the i's and cross the t's*.

2. I was in a hurry to get this letter to the lawyer. It was more important to get it mailed today than to *dot the i's and cross the t's*.

The expression probably originates from the idea of being careful to complete the letters "i" and "t" in cursive handwriting to ensure they are clearly identifiable from each other.

DOWN AND OUT

poor

1. Years ago Sam was *down and out*. He had no job and no money.

2. This is a shelter for the *down and out* of the city. The homeless can come here for a hot meal and a place to sleep at night.

The expression suggests the idea of being down at the bottom of society and out of luck.

DOWN IN THE DUMPS
depressed

1. I'm not feeling very cheerful these days. I've been *down in the dumps* for a while.

2. We've been *down in the dumps* ever since our pet cat died. I wonder if getting a new kitten would make us feel better.

Synonyms: *blue; down in the mouth*

DOWN IN THE MOUTH
unhappy

1. Jeff has been *down in the mouth* since he lost his job.

2. You look so sad. Why so *down in the mouth?*

Synonyms: *blue; down in the dumps*

A reference to the way one's mouth turns downward when one is sad.

DOWN TO EARTH
practical and rational; unpretentious

1. The boss always listens to Ralph's suggestions because his ideas are reasonable and *down-to-earth.*

2. John is just the kind of young man a girl's parents want her to marry. He's so practical and *down-to-earth* about everything.

Synonym: *both feet on the ground*

Antonym: *head in the clouds*

The expression suggests one has one's feet firmly planted on solid ground rather than having unrealistic ideas or flighty behavior.

DOWN TO THE WIRE
to the deadline

1. The newspaper article was due no later than 4 o'clock and the editor got it in at exactly 3:59. He went right *down to the wire.*

2. Some students write their best research papers if they wait until the night before they are due. They leave them until they are *down to the wire.*

Synonym: *eleventh hour*

Compare to: *in the nick of time; under the wire*

Whereas *eleventh hour* means late, *down to the wire, under the wire* and *in the nick of time* convey the sense of being just barely in time.

DRAW A BLANK
to be unable to remember

1. Charles *drew a blank* when he tried to remember the date of his wedding anniversary. He had to ask his wife when it was.

2. Andrea always *draws a blank* when she runs into people she doesn't know very well. She's never quite sure she has met them before.

Used at least since the 16th century, this idiom originally referred to lottery tickets. One who *drew a blank* had a ticket worth nothing.

DRAW THE LINE AT (SOMETHING)
to not allow something beyond a certain acceptable point

1. Their parents let them go out on weekend nights, but they *draw the line* at letting them go out on school nights.

2. You may buy a car with your savings, but not a motorcycle. I'm going to *draw the line at* that.

The expression suggests the idea of drawing a line to mark an outer limit.

DRESSED TO KILL
dressed to make a strong impression, usually in fancy or stylish clothes

1. I was very embarrassed when I walked into the party thinking it was informal and found that everyone except me was *dressed to kill.*

2. Marjorie wanted to make a lasting impression on John. When he arrived to take her out, she was *dressed to kill.*

DROP IN THE BUCKET, A
an extremely small amount compared to the whole, usually much less than what is needed or wanted

1. We need to raise over one million dollars to fund the new Center for AIDS Research. The thousand dollars we have already collected is just a *drop in the bucket.*

2. What he paid me is only a *drop in the bucket* compared to what he owes me.

DRUM (SOMEONE)/GET DRUMMED OUT OF THE CORPS
to expel someone from a group or organization

1. If I suggested to the boss that the company pay for the Christmas party, he'd probably fire me. *I'd get drummed out of the corps.*

2. When Henry recommended that the men's club should admit women as members, they *drummed him out of the corps.*

The expression originates from a military setting where, when someone left the corps in disgrace, he or she was escorted out with a drum roll. Its usage includes any group and carries with it a sense of disgrace or rejection.

DUTCH TREAT {GO DUTCH}

each person pays for himself or herself; to share the cost

1. Larry didn t have enough money to pay for both his and Mary's dinner, so they went *Dutch treat*.

2. When I go out to lunch with my colleagues at work, each of us pays for herself. We *go Dutch*.

Antonym: *treat*

Whereas the basic expression *treat* means to pay for someone else, *Dutch treat* means that no one is treating. *Dutch treat is* often used in spoken English; in formal, written English, one often sees an expression like "no-host lunch" to indicate that each person pays for his or her own meal.

DYED IN THE WOOL

having a trait that is thoroughly ingrained or basic to one's nature

1. Ron and Ted love baseball. They know all the players on every team and all the statistics about each one. They are *dyed-in-the-wool* baseball fans.

2. No one works harder than Ann for the protection of the environment and wildlife. She is *dyed in the wool* as far as conservation goes.

E

EAGER BEAVER

a person who is very excited and enthusiastic about pursuing some activity

1. Paul just discovered jogging as a form of exercise, and he went out and bought new running shoes, a new tracksuit, and all the other gear that goes along with it. He's a real *eager beaver* about jogging.

2. Dieting must be done slowly and carefully. Don't be such an *eager beaver* to lose weight that you harm yourself by not eating anything.

The expression suggests the image of an anxiously working beaver, which is reputed to be an active, industrious animal. It has a slightly negative connotation, as of someone eager to impress others with his/her effort.

EAT CROW/HUMBLE PIE

to humble oneself because one has been proved wrong

1. Roger told his daughter that he didn t believe her. When he found out he was wrong, he had to *eat crow* and admit his mistake.

2. Cathy laughed at herself when she realized she was wrong and had spoken too quickly. "I jump to the wrong conclusions so often, I'm always eating *humble pie*," she said.

Synonym: *swallow (one's) pride*

EAT (ONE'S) HAT

to do something unpleasant in the case of being proven wrong

1. I don't believe the boss is going to give us an extra day off work at Christmas time. If he does, I'll *eat my hat.*

2. Matthew told me he would *eat his hat* if my favorite football team won the championship this year. He felt there was no possibility that they could win.

Compare to: *bet (one's) bottom dollar; bet (one's) boots*

EAT (ONE'S) HEART OUT

to suffer silently in a hopeless situation

1. Mike thought Sue would eventually marry him. Now that she has married Tony, he's *eating his heart out.*

2. Kevin tried to take the job that was rightfully mine by telling my boss that I had stolen money from the company. When I got the promotion anyway, all I could say to him was, "*Eat your heart out.*"

Compare to: *cry over spilled milk*

Whereas *cry over spilled milk* is to grieve over some event that has happened and cannot be changed, *eat one's heart out* is to grieve over an emotional situation that cannot be changed. The expression is also used in the command form by someone who has no sympathy for the grieving person (as in sentence 2).

EAT OUT OF (SOMEONE'S) HAND

to be submissive; to have someone *eating out of one's hand* means to get someone to be submissive

1. Jerry will do anything Lisa wants. She has him *eating out of her hand.*

2. The politician was so polished that had the crowd *eating out of his hand* by the end of his speech.

The expression originates from the idea that an animal that will eat out of one's hand is very tame. It connotes an unhealthy submissiveness.

EGG ON (ONE'S) FACE, HAVE

to be or appear to be embarrassed

1. I can tell by the way you look that you've been caught doing something naughty. You have *egg on your face.*

2. Andy sure had *egg on his face* when he realized he had made a fool of himself at the party.

ELEVENTH HOUR

late or last-minute

1. You certainly left making your decision to take this flight until the *eleventh hour.* You're lucky there were still seats available.

2. Don't wait until the *eleventh hour* to decide to see the doctor. If you do, you may find that it's too late.

Compare to: *down to the wire; in the nick of time*

Down to the wire and *in the nick of time* convey a greater sense of being just barely in time than the *eleventh hour.*

ETERNAL TRIANGLE

a situation in which two men love the same woman or two women love the same man

1. Both Nancy and Tanya love Victor. It's the age-old story of the *eternal triangle.*

2. Like many other romantic comedies, this film is about two men who fall in love with the same woman. It's a story of an *eternal triangle* gone awry.

The theme of the *eternal triangle* recurs throughout the literature of many cultures. The triangle (three people) is described as eternal because it is such a common situation.

EVERY TOM, DICK, AND HARRY

everyone

1. I know the car salesman made you think he was only offering a great deal to you, but in fact he has offered the same deal to *every Tom, Dick and Harry* that has walked into his showroom.

2. My rug is ruined. Every *Tom, Dick, and Harry* must have come through here with muddy shoes.

F

FACE THE MUSIC
to confront a difficult or unpleasant situation;
to accept the unpleasant consequences of one's
own actions

1. Jessica's parents have always made excuses for her
   bad behavior, but this time they told her they were
   not going to protect her, and that it was time she
   faced the music.

2. Paul took his parents' car without permission and
   put a big dent in it. He knew they would find out,
   so he decided he'd better *face the music* and tell the
   truth right away.

Compare to: *bite the bullet; take the bull by the horns*

Whereas *bite the bullet* focuses on preparing oneself to accept
physical pain or punishment, *face the music* focuses more on
accepting responsibility for some misdeed.

FAIR AND SQUARE
honest(ly)

1. Some people believe Andrew cheated, but he won the
   contest *fair and square*.

2. The working people didn't like the result of the
   election, but the opposition's candidate won
   honestly. The election was *fair and square*.

Compare to: *square deal*

In this expression, "square" means "right," or "not crooked."

FAIR SHAKE, GET/GIVE (SOMEONE) A
to give someone or something a chance to prove
itself

1. Don't dismiss this place so quickly; spend a little
   time getting used to it. *Give it a fair shake*.

2. You accuse me of stealing money from the store, but
   you don't give me a chance to tell you my side of the
   story. You're *not giving me a fair shake*.

FAIR TO MIDDLING
average; neither good nor bad

1. Don asked Melissa what she thought of the new
   restaurant. She told him she had been to better ones,
   but it wasn't bad. It was *fair to middling*.

2. Now that I'm beginning to get over my cold, I'm
   feeling *fair to middling*. I feel better than I did last
   week, but I still have a stuffy nose.

FAIR-WEATHER FRIEND
a person who is loyal in good times but not when
times are difficult

1. They thought Charles would help them the way
   they had helped him, but as soon as they asked for
   help, he disappeared. He turned out to be just *a fair-
   weather friend*.

2. Everybody wanted to be Sally's friend when she won
   the lottery. They weren t real friends, however; they
   were *fair-weather friends*.

The expression suggests the idea that someone is a friend only
when the weather is good, i.e., in good times.

FALL BY THE WAYSIDE
to drop out of the situation

1. When Greg had too many groceries to carry at once,
   he decided to keep what he needed for dinner that
   night and let the rest *fall by the wayside*.

2. Larry's parents told him to look to the future,
   concentrate on his long-term goals, and let the
   unimportant things *fall by the wayside*.

FALL FOR (SOMETHING)
to be deceived or believe an unlikely story

1. You want me to believe that you're late because you
   ran out of gasoline? You must think I'm a fool if you
   think I'm going to *fall for that*.

2. The judge said she didn't believe the thief's excuse
   that he simply forgot to pay for the food. The judge
   told him, "I'm not going to *fall for that* old story."

FALL FOR (SOMEONE)
to be in love with a person

1. Mike says that he *fell for* Rose the first time he saw
   her, and now they're getting married.

2. I know that man is handsome, but you don t want to
   fall for him—he's only in town for a week.

FALL OFF THE WAGON
to lose control of oneself and engage in a
compulsive behavior

1. She was doing well on her diet, but then she *fell off
   the wagon* and ate a gallon of ice cream.

2. If you're serious about staying sober, you shouldn't
   put yourself in situations where you might give in to
   temptation and *fall off the wagon*. Don't go to bars or
   parties where alcohol might be served.

This expression is generally used to refer to negative behaviors,
especially alcoholism.

FALL ON DEAF EARS

to be heard but ignored, or to be heard but to have no effect

1. Ashley went to the bank to beg for a loan because she had no job, but no one would listen to her. Her pleas *fell on deaf ears*.

2. The young husband tried to tell his wife why he was late getting home, but his excuse *fell on deaf ears*.

Compare to: *turn a deaf ear*.

The expression is used to describe spoken words. The listener is not really deaf, but acts that way. This idiom is essentially synonymous with *turn a deaf ear*, but whereas the request *falls on deaf ears*, the person who ignores the request *turns a deaf ear*.

FAR CRY FROM (SOMETHING)

much less than what was expected or anticipated

1. The bellboy took them to their hotel room. It was small, dark, and dirty—a *far cry from* what they were expecting.

2. Don't get your expectations up too high. What you get may be a *far cry from* what you want.

FAT CAT

a rich but usually lazy person

1. Now that Mr. Anderson is rich, he rides around town in a fancy car like a *fat cat* and has everyone else do the work.

2. Richard is such a *fat cat* businessman. He owns several supermarkets.

The expression is primarily used to describe a man (usually not a woman) who, although rich, is not seen as industrious. He has perhaps become wealthy through hard work but is now relaxing, or he has never had to work for his wealth.

FEATHER IN (ONE'S) CAP

an exceptional achievement

1. Cassandra managed through hard work to win a big contract for her company. It was a real *feather in her cap*.

2. The scholarship Lee won to attend the university was a *feather in his cap*.

Synonym: *something to crow about*

Antonym: *nothing to write home about*

Compare to: *feather (one's) nest*

The practice of placing a feather in one's cap is centuries old and appears to have been practiced in many different cultures. The feather was awarded and worn as a sign of a significant achievement by the wearer. In some cultures, such as 16th-century Hungary, it was a crime to wear a feather when one had not earned the right.

FEATHER (ONE'S) NEST

to build up one's riches, usually quietly and perhaps by some unethical method (sentence 2)

1. They have been working very hard these past few years, trying to *feather their nest* for retirement.

2. Mr. Jones has been *feathering his nest* with company money ever since he gained access to the safe. One of these days he's going to be found out and fired.

The expression suggests the idea of a bird making itself comfortable by adding feathers to its nest.

FEEL (SOMETHING) IN (ONE'S) BONES [HAVE A FEELING IN (ONE'S) BONES]

to sense something without being able to see, hear or feel it; to have a premonition

1. The sky may be clear, but it's going to rain. I can *feel it in my bones*.

2. Do you ever get the feeling that someone is watching you, even though you can't see him or her? You *get this feeling in your bones*.

FEEL THE PINCH

to have less money than one used to have, and less than one feels is necessary

1. The government raised taxes so much that even the rich began to *feel the pinch*.

2. When we had to pay for the university education of all three of our children at the same time, we really *felt the pinch*.

Synonym: *strapped for cash*

FIELD DAY

a wild and uncontrolled time; a time of especially pleasant or exciting action

1. The dogs got loose in Rachel's flowerbeds and had a *field day*. They virtually destroyed it.

2. The children had a *field day* spraying each other with the water hose. They were soaked within minutes.

FIGHT TOOTH AND NAIL

to fight fiercely; to fight with everything you have

1. The candidate said he would *fight tooth and nail* to get elected.

2. The two girls fought *tooth and nail* on the playground until a teacher interrupted.

The expression suggests that the fighter uses both teeth and fingernails or claws.

FILL/FIT THE BILL

to suit or satisfy a need

1. I'm looking for a lightweight gray suit. This one *fits the bill*—I can wear it year-round.

2. We thanked the real estate agent for trying to find us a house, but the ones she showed us just didn't *fill the bill*.

Synonym: *hit the spot*.

FILTHY RICH
extremely wealthy

1. He started the leading software company in the world. He's not just a little rich—he's *filthy rich*!
2. Whenever I buy a lottery ticket, I dream about what I would buy if I were *filthy rich*.

Antonym: *flat broke*

This expression arose from the idea that money was "filthy," or dirty. For some people, the idiom still carries a negative connotation. But for others, to be filthy rich is a dream.

FINE KETTLE OF FISH
a terrible mess

1. You borrowed money from the bank without telling me and we don't have enough to pay it back. This is *a fine kettle of fish* you've gotten us into.
2. Lois told her boss she could work on Saturday, but she forgot and promised her girlfriend she would help her move on Saturday. She had gotten herself into *a fine kettle of fish*.

The word "fine" is meant ironically.

FINE-TOOTH COMB
an imaginary device one uses to look for something very carefully

1. That professor goes over his students' research papers with *a fine-tooth comb* looking for mistakes. If there are any, he finds them.
2. The police examined the crime scene. They went over it with *a fine-tooth comb*, but they couldn't find any.

The expression suggests the idea that if something can be found (i.e., if it exists), it can be found by using a comb with very fine (i.e., closely spaced) teeth.

FIRST-RATE
best quality

1. George did a *first-rate* job on these drawings. I've never seen better.
2. Lynn's work is always the best. It's always *first-rate*.

Antonyms: *second-rate; third-rate*

FISH OUT OF WATER
a person who is uncomfortable in a situation or doesn't belong in a particular environment

1. Joe felt out of place at the fancy dinner dance, like *a fish out of water*.
2. You could tell they were uncomfortable making polite conversation with their son's friends. They were *fish out of water*.

Synonym: *out of (one's) element*

Antonym: *in (one's) element*

FISHY
looking or sounding suspicious

1. They won't say where they got their computer. Their story sounds *fishy* to me. I think they may have stolen it.
2. Someone called on the telephone telling me I had just won a free trip to Hawaii, but first I had to buy his or her product. It sounded pretty *fishy*, so I hung up.

FITS AND STARTS
in short bursts of motion or effort

1. When you play the violin, you must move the bow across the strings smoothly, not in *fits and starts*.
2. It took Sally a long time to finish her education. She pursued it in *fits and starts*.

FIX (SOMEONE'S) WAGON
to return an irritation caused by a person through some form of mild revenge

1. They think they can just come in here and order us around like servants. Well, *we'll fix their wagon*—next time they come, we'll ignore them.
2. That guy always parks his car in front of my driveway so I can't get out. Next time he does that, I'm going to let the air out of his tires. That'll *fix his wagon*.

Compare to: *give (someone) a taste of his own medicine; tit for tat*

FLASH IN THE PAN
a temporary or passing fancy; a fad or attraction that will fade quickly

1. I know he's been acclaimed as the best new playwright in the country, but I think he's just a *flash in the pan*. No one will know who he is by next year.
2. Short skirts are in fashion again, but I hope they're just a *flash in the pan*. I would hate to have to start wearing them again.

The expression comes from an old type of weapon, the flintlock musket. In these muskets, gunpowder was first ignited in a small depression or pan; this powder was supposed to cause the charge in the musket to explode. But sometimes the powder just burned harmlessly, giving off a flash but nothing more.

FLAT BROKE
have absolutely no money

1. I'd gladly loan you the money, but I can't because I'm *flat broke*.
2. They lost all their money in the stock market crash, and now they're *flat broke*.

Antonym: *filthy rich*

Compare to: *go broke*

FLY-BY-NIGHT

undependable; untrustworthy

1. The small trading company took in a lot of money from trusting investors and then closed up. It had been a *fly-by-night* operation.

2. Although Darlene had been working for the company for a few months and they had paid her, she still didn't trust them. She felt she was working for a *fly-by-night* company.

The expression suggests the idea that the operation closes up and flees under the cover of darkness rather than in the clear light of day.

FLY IN THE FACE OF (SOMETHING)

to go against something; to show disrespect for something or someone

1. John has decided not to go to college. It's a bad decision on his part. It *flies in the face of* all common sense.

2. If you marry someone your parents disapprove of so much, it will *fly in the face of everything* they want for you.

FLY IN THE OINTMENT

an unpleasant element in an otherwise pleasant situation

1. The trip was all planned. Our tickets were paid for. Then the boss said we had an unexpected increase in orders and that we would have to take our vacation another time. What a *fly in the ointment*!

2. I'm not sure, but I think we have a *fly in the ointment*. I know I said I would take you to the ball game this weekend, but I remembered this morning that I already offered to give my extra ticket to someone at work.

FLY OFF THE HANDLE

to suddenly become very angry

1. When Dana came home and found that her husband had painted the house bright pink without asking her, she *flew off the handle*. She was so angry that she painted it white again.

2. Nathan has a very short temper. He gets angry and *flies off the handle* for the slightest reason.

Synonyms: *blow (one's) stack; see red*

FLY THE COOP

to escape

1. The prisoner waited until the guards were fast asleep. He unlocked his cell door with a hairpin and *flew the coop.*

2. The man felt trapped in a dead-end job. All he wanted to do was *fly the coop.*

The expression is usually used in connection with being in jail (sentence 1) but can also be used figuratively (sentence 2). It is a reference to captured birds escaping when their cage (coop) is opened.

FOLLOW IN (SOMEONE'S) FOOTSTEPS

to follow the same career or lifestyle as someone else

1. James was a convicted thief who had spent years in jail. He didn't want his son to *follow in his footsteps.*

2. The daughter had always admired her mother's work helping the poor. From an early age she was determined to *follow in her mother's footsteps.*

Compare to: *chip off the old block*

The *someone* in the expression is traditionally, but not necessarily, a parent.

FOOD FOR THOUGHT

something to think about

1. When asked about a tax increase on gasoline to help pay for public education, the governor said he hadn't considered that kind of tax, but he said it certainly was *food for thought.*

2. Sarah read the book that had been recommended to her and found that it contained a lot of *food for thought.*

Compare to: *chew it over*

In use since the early 1800s, this idiom refers metaphorically to the idea that the mind 'chews' on thought like the mouth chews on food.

FOOL AROUND

to play, or to not be serious about an activity

1. Don't worry about the boys playing in the back yard—I can see them through the window. They're just *fooling around.*

2. If you want to pass history class, you'll have to study hard and not *fool around.*

Synonyms: *horse around, clown around, monkey around*

This expression can be neutral (sentence 1) or slightly negative (sentence 2).

FOOL'S GOLD

something that appears to have great value but is in fact a cheap imitation

1. The scientists thought they had discovered a source of cheap energy through their experiments, but it later proved to be nothing but *fool's gold.*

2. Don't invest all your money in a fancy scheme that seems too good to be true. All you'll end up with is *fool's gold.*

The expression originates from miners who often found veins of a gold-colored substance called pyrite, which they mistook for gold.

FOOTLOOSE AND FANCY-FREE

able to go anywhere and do anything that one wants; carefree

1. Michael didn't want to get married. He wanted to remain *footloose and fancy-free*.

2. When they finished college, they spent a year traveling though Europe with their backpacks and sleeping bags. They just wanted some time to be *footloose and fancy-free*.

The expression literally means one's foot is not tied down and one can freely follow one's impulses (fancy).

FORBIDDEN FRUIT

something that one cannot have

1. When people can readily have something, they don't want it. But when you tell them they can t have it, that's all they want. There's nothing like the attraction of *forbidden fruit*.

2. Jody's parents told her not to date Dennis because they think he might be a bad influence on her. But now that they've made him *forbidden fruit,* he's the only boy who interests her.

The expression originates from the Biblical story of Adam and Eve, where God forbade Adam and Eve to eat the fruit from one of the trees in the Garden of Eden. This made the fruit so tempting that they were unable to resist eating it.

FORCE TO BE RECKONED WITH, A

something or someone whose influence or power must be considered

1. I underestimated the influence of Mr. Franklin in this company. He certainly is *a force to be reckoned with*.

2. Catherine seemed to be a gentle person, but when Roger angered her, she lashed out at him. He discovered she was *a force to be reckoned with*.

FOR CRYING OUT LOUD

an expletive that means "This is ridiculous!" or "I've had enough!" It carries no literal meaning of its own, but expresses a strong degree of exasperation.

1. All you do is complain. *For crying out loud,* can't you give us some peace and quiet for a while?

2. The children were jumping around, chasing after each other and running around their mother until she couldn't stand it anymore. She said to them, "Stop playing around, *for crying out loud.*"

Synonyms: *for goodness' sake!; for heaven's sake!*

FOR GOODNESS' SAKE

an expletive that means "This is ridiculous!" or "I've had enough!" It carries no literal meaning of its own, but expresses a strong degree of exasperation

1. This traffic is making me crazy! *For goodness' sake*, can't we go any faster?

2. *For goodness' sake*, why didn't we order movie tickets ahead of time? The line is so long that we'll probably miss the beginning!

Synonyms: *for crying out loud!; for heaven's sake!*

FOR HEAVEN'S SAKE

an expletive that means "This is ridiculous!" or "I've had enough!" It carries no literal meaning of its own, but expresses a strong degree of exasperation

1. *For heaven's sake*, why are you up so early? Go back to bed, so I can sleep!

2. *For heaven's sake*, how can it be so hot outside? I wish we had air conditioning.

Synonyms: *for goodness' sake!; for crying out loud!*

FOR THE BIRDS

a waste of time; mixed up or confused

1. We've been waiting in this line for movie tickets over four hours. Let's go home. This is *for the birds*.

2. The boss wants us to work every Saturday for the next three months without pay. He's *for the birds*.

Synonyms: *all wet* (sentence 1)*; out to lunch* (sentence 2)

FORTY WINKS

a short sleep, usually during the day

1. There's a little time before lunch. I think I'm going to lie down for a while and catch *forty winks*.

2. My husband always likes to put his feet up in the easy chair and get *forty winks* before supper.

FOURTH-RATE

of inferior quality; not the best

1. The company introduced a new car model, but the production quality is still *fourth-rate*, like all their other cars.

2. My assessment is that he's a *fourth-rate* man with a first-rate education. He's been well trained, but I don't think he understands what our company's about.

Antonym: *first-rate*

Synonyms: *second-rate; third-rate*

Expressions using *rate* generally go only as far as *fourth-rate*. *Second-, third-,* and *fourth-rate* are synonymous. There are no degrees of inferiority. They are all opposites of *first-rate*.

from the beginning; from the outset

1. Their new employee caused trouble *from day one*. They fired him only a month after hiring him.

2. *From day one*, I knew she was the girl for me. It really was a case of love at first sight.

Synonym: *from the word go*

from the beginning

1. I didn't understand a thing from the moment the math teacher opened his mouth. I was lost *from the word go.*

2. The candidate was never half-hearted about winning. She was serious *from the word go.*

Synonym: *from day one*

The expression suggests a race in which the beginning is marked by the word go.

to proceed with maximum power and speed

1. We finally got the money from the bank to build our house, and now we're ready to go *full steam ahead.*

2. Patrick wasn't fully aware of how bad the situation was, but he charged in *full steam ahead* anyway.

The expression suggests the idea that when a steam engine is full of steam, it operates at maximum power.

G

GET A HANDLE ON (SOMETHING)

to find a way to deal with a problem or difficult situation

1. I'm trying to *get a handle* on my job search, so I'm updating my resume and asking my old teachers for letters of recommendation.
2. Margaret's babysitting job was difficult at first, but she *got a handle on* the children after she promised to read them a story.

GET (A) HOLD OF (ONESELF)

to get control of oneself; stop being emotional

1. Stop crying, Mary. *Get a hold of yourself* and calm down.
2. The man narrowly missed hitting another car on the highway. Afterward, he pulled off the road to try to *get hold of himself.*

Compare to: *get it/(one's) act together; go to pieces*

The expression *get (a) hold of oneself* emphasizes emotional control whereas *get one's act together* emphasizes mental or physical control.

GET (A) HOLD OF (SOMEONE)

to contact someone or communicate with someone, usually by telephone

1. The real estate agent couldn't *get hold of* them before the house was sold to someone else. They never answered their phone.
2. The ambulance brought the little boy to the hospital, and the doctor *got a hold of* the boy's parents before he operated.

GET (A) HOLD OF (SOMETHING)

to acquire or obtain something

1. I was able to *get hold of* a copy of the magazine, but it was the last one.
2. Sarah was very lucky to *get a hold of* an extra ticket to the ballgame.

The expression is used to describe something that is somewhat difficult to acquire, perhaps because it is rare.

GET A LEG UP

to make a good start on some activity or project

1. It took a long time, but you've finally *got a leg up* on your college degree. It shouldn't take you much longer to finish.
2. I'm going to *get a leg up* on next year's budget by planning several months in advance.

This expression originally meant "to be lifted onto a horse," and can indicate getting ahead of other people.

GET A MOVE ON

to hurry

1. *Get a move on!* Everyone is waiting for you.
2. We asked the waiter to bring our check twenty minutes ago. I sure wish that he would *get a move on!*

Synonyms: *shake a leg!; step on it!*

This expression can be used as a verb or as a command to another person.

GET A WORD IN EDGEWISE

to insert a word or sentence into an otherwise one-sided conversation

1. Elizabeth talked on and on. No one else got a chance to tell her what he or she thought because they couldn t *get a word in edgewise.*
2. Jerry finally *got a word in edgewise* when Tony stopped talking to take a drink.

The word *edgewise* means to turn something to its narrowest dimension. The expression suggests that one must put one's words *edgewise* in order to squeeze them into a conversation where words are run together very tightly. The expression is usually used in the negative, *can't get a word in edgewise,* meaning that one is unable to get into the conversation because someone else is doing all the talking.

GET BY

to just barely manage, financially (sentence 1) or with one's work or responsibilities (sentence 2)

1. We're *getting by* now, but if we get an unexpected bill it would bankrupt us.
2. I'm *getting by* the best way I know how: by working hard.

Synonyms: *keep one's head above water; make ends meet*

GET CAUGHT/BE LEFT HOLDING THE BAG [LEAVE (SOMEONE) HOLDING THE BAG]

to make someone the scapegoat; to be blamed for something that was not one's fault or was only partly one's fault

1. The other team members left, Bill *was left holding the bag,* trying to explain a bad project.
2. Christine helped Tim invent a scheme to cheat people out of their money and it went wrong. She left town and Tim *got caught holding the bag.*

Compare to: *leave (someone) in the lurch*

Leave someone in the lurch is usually applied more generally to any number of situations involving responsibility whereas leave *someone holding the bag is* usually applied to a situation involving theft in which one person is literally left holding (or caught with) the stolen goods.

GET DOWN TO BRASS TACKS/BUSINESS/ THE NITTY GRITTY

to get serious or practical about something

1. I think we've fooled around with this plan long enough. It's time to *get down to brass tacks*.

2. The meeting should have started fifteen minutes ago. I have another appointment in an hour, and I wish we would *get down to business*.

3. Your ideas in this report are hard to understand. Why not take out all the useless information and *get down to the nitty gritty*?

Compare to: (sentence 1) *talk turkey;* (sentence 2) *get the show on the road*

To *get down to business* means to get serious and start. To *get down to the nitty gritty* means to get to the basic issue or problem.

GET IT IN THE NECK

to receive something unpleasant, such as criticism or punishment

1. I thought I was doing a fine job until I was fired because the boss didn't like my work. I sure *got it in the neck*.

2. Frank thought they were the best of friends. Then one day for no apparent reason, she stopped speaking to him. He really *got it in the neck*

The *it* in the expression probably refers to a foot or fist. The expression suggests getting kicked or hit in the neck.

GET OFF (ONE'S) HIGH HORSE

to stop acting superior

1. Ted really acts like he thinks he's the boss around here. He'd better *get off his high horse* pretty soon or he'll have no friends.

2. Who do you think you are coming in here and ordering me around like this? *Get off your high horse!*

The expression originates from the custom of high-ranking officials traveling on horseback, while commoners walked. The physical height of being up on the horse is equated with being in a superior position.

GET OFF/GO SCOT-FREE

to escape the proper or expected punishment; to be acquitted of a crime

1. Everyone knew the man had committed the crime, but he was found not guilty on a technicality and never spent a day in jail. He *got off scot-free*.

2. The thief had been caught too many times, but this time he would not *go scot-free*. He would spend years in prison.

GET (ONE'S) ACT/IT TOGETHER

to get control of oneself mentally or physically; to get organized

1. Virginia had been lazy on the job for some time. Her boss told her she had better *get her act together* or she would be looking for another job soon.

2. I don't know where my mind is these days—I feel so disorganized. I can't seem to *get it together*.

Synonyms: *on the ball; get a hold of (oneself)*

On the ball is a more subtle way of expressing someone's lack of mental control than *get one's act together*. *Get one's act together* emphasizes mental or physical control, whereas *get a hold of oneself* emphasizes emotional control.

GET (ONE'S) SECOND WIND

to get a second burst of energy

1. The dancers had to stop for a few minutes to take a rest. When they *got their second wind,* they started to dance again.

2. The candidate took the weekend off from campaigning because he was mentally exhausted. He told reporters that he would be back on the campaign trail after he *got his second wind*.

The expression suggests that when a person gets out of breath *(wind)*, he/she can get a second one in order to continue. It can be used literally (sentence 1) or figuratively (sentence 2).

GET (SOMEONE'S) DANDER/HACKLES UP

to irritate or anger moderately

1. I don't like that man. Perhaps it's the way he talks to me or the way he acts around us—he sure *gets my dander up*.

2. Our neighbors are extremely messy and loud. They *get my hackles up*.

Synonyms: *rub (someone) the wrong way; set (someone's) teeth on edge; get (someone's) goat; bug*

Whereas *bug* means to annoy harmlessly or perhaps humorously, *get one's dander up* means to irritate in earnest.

GET (SOMEONE'S) GOAT

to irritate or annoy someone

1. I can't believe the boss is giving Judith the day before Christmas off, when he refused to let me take the day off. That really *gets my goat!*

2. The one thing that really *gets my husband's goat* is when he finds a parking place and someone else comes along and steals it.

Compare to: *get (one's) dander up; bug*

GET (SOMETHING) OFF (ONE'S) CHEST
to disclose or talk about something that is bothering or worrying one

1. I've had something on my mind all day that I just have to tell you. I will feel better when I *get it off my chest.*

2. You look very troubled about something. Why don't you talk about it and *get it off your chest?*

The idiom suggests that a bothersome concern weighs down one's chest or heart and that talking about it relieves the weight.

GET/HIT (SOMETHING) ON THE NOSE
to do or understand something perfectly

1. That's the right answer! You really *got it on the nose.*

2. Joannie's argument made perfect sense to me—she really *hit it on the nose.*

GET (SOMETHING) THROUGH (ONE'S) HEAD
to understand something that is difficult, especially because it is a shock, unwanted, or unexpected

1. How many times do I have to tell you, I'm not going back to college? When will you *get it through your head* that I want to go to work instead?

2. Tom couldn t seem to *get it through his head* that his company was letting him go after so many years of faithful service.

Compare to: *get the message*

The expression is usually used in a negative sense to describe how difficult it is to understand or accept something.

GET/GIVE THE GO-AHEAD
to receive or grant permission to proceed

1. The planning stage of the project was complete and we *got the go-ahead* to start construction.

2. The staff *got the go-ahead* from their boss to organize a birthday party for their colleague.

Synonym: *get/give (someone) the green light*

GET THE MESSAGE
to understand something that is only hinted at, perhaps because it is unpleasant

1. You can stop hinting that you don't want my company. I *get the message*, and I won t bother you again.

2. Jacqueline never answered the many letters the young man sent to her. She wondered when he would *get the message* that she wasn t interested in hearing from him.

Compare to: *get (something) through (one's) head*

GET THIS SHOW ON THE ROAD
to get started

1. We've been waiting for hours, and I'm ready to get started. Let's *get the show on the road.*

2. I can't wait any longer. If we don't *get the show on the road,* I'm going to have to schedule this meeting for another day.

Compare to: *get down to business*

GET TO THE BOTTOM OF (SOMETHING)
to understand something completely by sorting through all the facts or information

1. The detective had all the facts, but he couldn t piece them together yet. He wasn't certain what had happened, but he knew he would eventually *get to the bottom of it.*

2. Mark's parents could tell he was getting into some kind of trouble. They confronted him and said they wanted to *get to the bottom of* the situation.

The expression suggests the idea of a container (a situation) full of information or facts. Only the few facts on top are clear and they may not make much sense. When one finally *gets to the bottom* of the container (the situation), one will have gone through all the information and have a thorough understanding of how all the facts fit together.

GET TO THE POINT
to speak or write concisely and directly

1. That fellow never wastes your time talking about unimportant things. He immediately *gets to the point.*

2. People seem to *get to the point* much more quickly when they write e-mail compared to a traditional letter.

Antonyms: *beat around the bush; hem and haw*

GET-UP-AND-GO
physical energy

1. I've been so tired lately. I don't have any energy. I've lost my *get-up-and-go.*

2. This breakfast cereal claims that it gives you enough *get-up-and-go* to last you until lunchtime.

3. Contrary to popular belief, moderate exercise stimulates a person to have more *get up and go.* It doesn't fatigue the body.

GET UP ON THE WRONG SIDE OF THE BED
to be in a bad mood from the beginning of the day

1. Don't be upset that Peggy got angry with you; she'll cool off soon. She always has a short temper when she *gets up on the wrong side of the bed.*

2. I'm sorry I yelled at you. I must have *gotten up on the wrong side of the bed.*

Originally this phrase was "got up left foot forward" and dates back to the ancient Romans. In their time, the left side of anything was seen as sinister or unlucky, and Romans believed it was bad luck to put the left foot down first when getting out of bed. The idea that left is bad continued for centuries and eventually the word *left* was replaced with *wrong.*

GET/GIVE (SOMEONE/SOMETHING) SHORT SHRIFT
to make quick work of something or to give little time to someone

1. The secretary preferred working with people directly. She was an excellent secretary but she *gave short shrift* to typing up notes and preparing reports.

2. I haven't much time for incompetent fools like Sam. I *gave him short shrift* when he came in here asking for a pay raise.

The expression conveys a negative feeling about someone or something. They are thought of as unworthy of much time or consideration.

GET/GIVE (SOMEONE) THE COLD SHOULDER
to ignore someone intentionally

1. Margie and Steve used to be close friends, but now every time they meet, *she gives him the cold shoulder.*

2. When we bought our new house, we thought everyone would welcome us to the neighborhood. But people *give us the cold shoulder* when we try to be friendly and neighborly.

Synonym: *turn up (one's) nose at (someone/something)*

Whereas *give someone the cold shoulder* is used only with people, *turn up one's nose* can be applied to both people and things.

GET/GIVE (SOMEONE) THE GO-AHEAD
to get or give permission to proceed

1. The kids asked their mother for permission to set up a lemonade stand. Her lemon tree was full of lemons, so she *gave them the go-ahead.*

2. Playing baseball in the middle of the work day sounds like a great idea, but you should probably *get the go-ahead* from our boss before we start.

Synonym: *get/give (someone) the green light*

GET/GIVE (SOMEONE) THE GREEN LIGHT
to get or give permission to proceed

1. The planning stage of the project was complete and we *got the green light* to start construction.

2. The boss *gave them the green light* to order all the equipment they needed.

Synonym: *give/get (someone) the go-ahead*

This expression comes from the green light on a stop light, which indicates that cars can move forward.

GET/GIVE (SOMEONE) THE SACK
to be fired from one's job

1. John lost his job yesterday. He *got the sack.*

2. Marie has two small children to support. You can't just *give her the sack.* What is she going to do for money?

3. I *was sacked* from my last job for showing up late every day.

Compare to: *pink slip*

GET/GIVE (SOMEONE) THE SHORT END OF THE STICK
to get (give someone) the unfair or less advantageous part of a deal or arrangement

1. Martha agreed to babysit the children while Henry went shopping. Martha had much more work to do than Henry did. She *got the short end of the stick.*

2. Look out for your interests and speak up if you think you're getting an unfair deal. Don't let them *give you the short end of the stick.*

GET/GIVE (SOMEONE) THE THIRD DEGREE
to be questioned in great detail

1. My parents didn't believe that I'd spent the evening at the library. They *gave me the third degree,* questioning me about when I had arrived and left and what I'd done while I was there.

2. When it was revealed that the candidate had been arrested some years before, he *got the third degree* from the newspaper reporters. He had to answer question after question.

GET/HAVE (SOMETHING) DOWN PAT
to do something repeatedly until one knows how to do it without a mistake; to perfect an activity

1. Lynn worked on her dance routine until she could practically do it in her sleep. She *had it down pat.*

2. Practice saying your speech again and again. I want to be sure you *get it down pat.*

GET/LEND (SOMEONE) A HAND
to help someone

1. I need some help lifting these boxes. Who can *give me a hand*?

2. They *gave him a hand* with his rent and utility bills while he was unemployed.

The expression suggests that by giving someone a hand, one helps that person do more work than he could do with his own two hands. The expression is usually used in the sense of helping someone physically (sentence 1) but it can also be used in a financial sense (sentence 2).

GIFT OF GAB, THE
the ability to speak easily and well

1. We always enjoy listening to Uncle Charlie's stories. He really knows how to tell good ones—he's got *the gift of gab*.

2. I'm not much of a talker. I wasn't blessed with *the gift of gab*.

Compare to: *talk a blue streak*

The expression is used humorously or with admiration. It suggests that being able to speak *(gab)* is a welcome trait *(gift)*. The word *gab* is probably an Old English variation of the Scottish word 'gob,' which means 'mouth' or 'beak.'

GIVE IN
to surrender

1. The workers refused to *give in* and accept the unfair contract, so the strike continued.

2. The parents tried to resist their children's pleas for sweets, but the kids were so cute that the parents were forced to *give in*.

Similar to: *cry uncle; knuckle under*

GIVE (ONE'S) RIGHT (BODY PART) FOR/TO DO (SOMETHING)
to want something very much

1. I want that car so badly. I'd *give my right arm for* that car.

2. Veronica wants so badly to spend her vacation on the beach, she said she'd *give her right leg to* go to Hawaii.

The expression suggests that one wants something so much that one is willing to give an essential part of one's body for it.

GIVE (SOMEONE) A HARD TIME
to be difficult with someone; to give someone unnecessary difficulty

1. Patricia had not done a good job on the report, and she thought her boss would just ask her to redo it. Instead, *gave her a hard time* and wouldn't stop talking about it. He *gave her a hard time* about the report.

2. The students *gave the new teacher a hard time* on his first day. They dropped their books, passed notes while he was talking, and were generally uncooperative.

GIVE (SOMEONE) A PIECE OF (ONE'S) MIND
to confront someone who has behaved badly

1. Joan was upset with Bill and she told him just what she thought of him. She really *gave him a piece of her mind*.

2. I can't believe that they let their dog loose in my garden. I'm going over there right now to tell them that if I find that dog in my yard again, I'll call the police. I'm going to *give them a piece of my mind!*

Synonyms: *read (someone) the riot act; chew (someone) out; rake (someone) over the coals; speak (one's) piece*

GIVE (SOMEONE) A RING
to call someone on the telephone

1. When Sally arrived, she found a telephone in the airport and *gave her mother a ring*.

2. I'll be home by the phone all morning. *Give me a ring* when you get a chance.

Refers to the ringing of a telephone when it receives a call.

GIVE (SOMEONE) A SNOW JOB
to give someone a description of something or someone that is unrealistically attractive and positive

1. The English teacher was trying to find students to help with the publication of the school newspaper. She *gave us a snow job* about how much fun it would be and how little work it was—in fact, it was very hard work.

2. Richard tried to get Marsha to go out with his friend Don. Richard told Marsha that Don was good-looking, had a great personality and was rich. Richard *gave Marsha a snow job*, because Don turned out to be none of those things.

Synonyms: *sales pitch; con job; song and dance; pull the wool over (someone's) eyes*

GIVE (SOMEONE) A/SOME SONG AND DANCE
to give someone an overly dramatic or unbelievable excuse

1. Don't *give me a song and dance* about how difficult it was for you to get this work done on time—I know you've been goofing off.

2. We went to collect the rent from Paul, but *he gave us some song and dance* about not having the money right now.

Synonyms: *pull the wool over (someone's) eyes; cock and bull story; snow job*

GIVE (SOMEONE) A TASTE OF (HIS/HER) OWN MEDICINE

to treat someone the same way they treat others (especially when they are strict, unfair, or unkind)

1. She has treated everyone very unfairly. I wish that someone would *give her a taste of her own medicine*.

2. He always criticizes his colleagues for making careless mistakes. So after he accidentally started a fire in the office, they were really able to *give him a taste of his own medicine*.

Similar to: *fix (someone's) wagon; tit for tat*

GIVE (SOMEONE/SOMETHING) A WIDE BERTH

to allow a lot of space between oneself and someone or something else when passing

1. The children never walked on the south side of the road because they would have had to walk right past a frightening guard dog. They *gave that dog a wide berth*.

2. They couldn't tell if the driver was ready to back the truck up or whether he even saw them in his rear-view mirror. Just to be safe, they *gave the truck a wide berth* when they crossed the street behind it.

The expression probably originates from the 18th-century meaning of *berth*: sufficient sea-room for one ship to pass another.

GIVE (SOMEONE) THE COLD SHOULDER

to be unfriendly to somebody

1. Audrey tried to make up with Josh after their fight, but Josh didn't respond. He *gave her the cold shoulder*.

2. Beatrice was forced to find a new photography club when the members of her old club *gave her the cold shoulder*. They wouldn't talk to her at all.

GIVE (SOMEONE) THE SHIRT OFF (ONE'S) BACK

to give (figuratively) someone all one's possessions; to be very generous

1. The young woman's parents had denied themselves luxuries and vacations to provide for her. They had *given her the shirts off their backs* to give her a good life.

2. I know I can always depend on my friend Henry. I can call him whenever I need help. .

The expression suggests that one would give someone all one's money and possessions down even to the shirt one is wearing.

GO AGAINST THE GRAIN

to be contrary to someone's nature

1. I'll get you out of trouble this one time, but don't ask me to do it again. It *goes against the grain* for me to help you when you should take responsibility for your own actions.

2. Terry noticed that the cashier in the store had given him too much change, and he went back immediately to return it. It would have *gone against the grain* for Terry to keep the money.

The expression originates from the idea that sawing wood against the grain (the natural direction of wood growth) is difficult.

GO AROUND IN CIRCLES

to be confused or lost; to make no progress

1. The directions to Arthur's house were so muddled and confused, he had us lost and *going around in circles*.

2. The instructions for how to put the toy together were not explained clearly at all. Mary *went around in circles* trying to figure them out.

GO BANANAS [DRIVE (SOMEONE) BANANAS]

to go crazy; to no longer be able to cope with a situation. To *drive someone bananas* means to annoy or irritate someone.

1. I'll *go bananas* if I have to sit for a whole evening and listen to that man talk on and on about his coin collection. It's boring to everyone but him.

2. The woman told her husband that the children were *driving her bananas*. He would have to look after them for the evening while she went out to a movie with some friends.

Synonyms: *at the end of (one's) rope; at (one's) wits' end*

GO BROKE

to run out of money completely; to become penniless

1. You can *go broke* buying Christmas presents for your children with today's high prices!

2. The drugstore on the corner is going out of business next week. The owner *went broke*.

Compare to: *flat broke*

GO FOR BROKE

to risk everything

1. The gambler was down to his last hundred dollars. He decided to *go for broke*, and he put the last of his money on one hand of cards.

2. Jan *went for broke* and invested all her money in the playwright's new play. If it was a success, she would be rich. If it was a flop, she would be penniless.

GO HAYWIRE
to malfunction; to break down

1. The robot worked fine until it tried to maneuver around the corner and *went haywire*. Its arms started to spin around, its head fell off, and it started shooting sparks out of its control panel.
2. When the man heard that his doctor's appointment was cancelled, he *went haywire*. He shouted that he would never go to the doctor again, and left.

Similar to: *at the end of (one's) rope; go bananas; at (one's) wits' end; go to pieces.*

Go *haywire is* generally applied to machines, whereas *go bananas* is more humorous and is restricted to people.

GO IT ALONE
to travel some path or do some activity by oneself, often something dangerous or risky

1. I tried to *go it alone* on completing the project, but I just couldn't do it. I had to get someone to help me.
2. The mountain climber said his route up the mountain is too dangerous for anyone but the most experienced person, so he won't take anyone with him. He is *going it alone.*

GO OFF HALF-COCKED
to do or say something in haste or without adequate planning or preparation

1. I know your daughter is late, but before you *go off half-cocked*, give her a chance to tell you her side of the story.
2. Dick thought up a scheme to get rich quick, but he didn't put much planning into it. He *went off half-cocked*, got into financial trouble, and made a fool of himself.

The expression probably originates from the idea of a gun misfiring when it is only half-cocked (as opposed to fully cocked), and therefore not fully ready to be fired.

GO OFF THE DEEP END
to become deeply involved with someone or something before one is ready; to go crazy

1. Peter *went off the deep end* when he met Marilyn. After just two months, they are already engaged to be married.
2. Sometimes it's easy to get overly excited about something new and different and *go off the deep end.*

The expression suggests the idea of plunging into the deep end of a swimming pool and being in over one's head.

GO OUT ON A LIMB
to take a risk

1. You have embarrassed and disappointed me several times before. Don t ask me to *go out on a limb* for you again.
2. They *went out on a limb* and lent him the money he asked for even though he was a poor risk. They could have lost all their money.

Synonym: *stick (one's) neck out*

The expression suggests that going out on a tree branch that might break is risky. The expression, however, is not used to describe physical risk.

GO OVER WITH A BANG
to be extremely successful

1. The author's latest book was more popular than he expected. In fact, it *went over with a bang.*
2. The fast-food restaurant's new chicken sandwich *went over with a bang.* Everyone was asking for it.

Antonym: *go over like a lead balloon*

GO OVERBOARD
to go to excess; to do too much

1. You have to be careful when decorating cakes. It's easy to *go overboard* and put on too much icing, too many decorations and too many colors.
2. Don't go *overboard* on these new, modern styles. If you spend all your clothing allowance on them, you may be sorry when the fashion changes.

GO OVER LIKE A LEAD BALLOON
to be completely unsuccessful, contrary to expectations; to fail

1. The car company introduced a new model that was supposed to be amazing, but it *went over like a lead balloon.* Nobody wanted to buy it.
2. That actor has been in several great movies, but his latest film will probably *go over like a lead balloon.* It's just terrible!

GO TO PIECES
to fall apart physically or emotionally; to lose one's self-control

1. Roger thought he was no longer in love with Amanda, but when he saw her again he *went to pieces*. He sat down and cried.
2. I think you're going to need some new shoes soon. Those shoes you are wearing now are *going to pieces.*

The expression often describes uncontrollable crying.

GO TO POT/SEED

to fall into disrepair; to deteriorate from lack of attention

1. The house has really fallen into disrepair. It's too bad they let it *go to seed* like that.
2. George really neglects his appearance nowadays. He has let himself *go to pot*.

Synonym: *go to the dogs*

Go to seed originates in the idea that the fruit on plants 'goes to seed' if it is not picked when ripe.

GO TO THE DOGS

to fall into disrepair; to deteriorate

1. This restaurant used to be so fashionable and classy, but it has *gone to the dogs* since it changed management.
2. This neighborhood is *going to the dogs*—the homeowners aren't keeping their houses or their yards in good repair. It's a shame.

Synonyms: *go to pot/seed*

GO TO TOWN

To do something with maximum enthusiasm; to splurge

1. When they bought an old house, they added a new bathroom, a modern kitchen, a sun porch and two new bedrooms. They really *went to town* fixing up their house.
2. Since Alice was paying for her own wedding, she decided to spare no expense. She really wanted to *go to town* on her wedding arrangements.

Synonyms: *pull out all the stops; go whole hog; whole nine yards*

Go to town connotes more elegance than *go whole hog* or *(go the) whole nine yards*.

GO UP IN SMOKE

to disappear; to be ruined

1. Judy had planned carefully and put in a lot of time building her career. Then she made one foolish mistake, and saw all her hard work *go up in smoke*.
2. The family managed to escape from the burning house. As they stood outside in the cold, they watched their house *go up in smoke*.
3. Larry expected to finish college and start a small company of his own, but all his plans *went up in smoke* when he lost his scholarship.

The expression suggests the idea of being burned. It is usually used figuratively to describe work (sentence 1) or plans (sentence 3) but it can be used literally (sentence 2).

GO WHOLE HOG

to spare nothing; to do something with maximum enthusiasm

1. The company *went whole hog* on the luncheon. They included both soup and salad on the menu, a choice of three main dishes and several desserts, and they paid for all the drinks, too.
2. When it comes to outfitting my car, I believe in *going whole hog*. I always get cruise control, extra padded seats, stereo, all the little luxuries.

Synonyms: *pull out all the stops; go to town; whole nine yards*

The expression does not convey the same sense of elegance as *go to town* does.

GO WITH THE FLOW

to take a relaxed attitude towards life

1. Life has its ups and downs. You shouldn't spend your time worrying. Just *go with the flow*.
2. I wish I could learn to *go with the flow* more. Whenever I have a problem at school, I get all stressed out.

Similar to: *like water off a duck's back; roll with the punches; take (something) in stride*

GOLDEN AGE

a time when something is at its best

1. The 1930s were the *golden age* of radio, when everyone gathered around in the evenings to listen. After television took over, radio became secondary.
2. The *golden* age of American literature began at the turn of the 20th century.

The expression is usually used to refer to the past.

GOOD EGG

a person who is basically good or sound, but who may be slightly peculiar or idiosyncratic

1. Sometimes Tim seems a little strange, but he really is *a good egg*.
2. George knew that Stuart was too cautious to drink very much, so George asked him to be *a good egg* and drive him home.

GOOD GRIEF!

an expletive that means "This is ridiculous!" or "I've had enough!"

1. *Good grief!* All you do is complain.
2. The children were jumping around, chasing after each other, and running around their mother until she couldn't stand it anymore. She lost her temper and yelled, "*Good grief!* I wish you would behave yourselves!"

Synonyms: *for crying out loud!; for goodness' sake!; for heaven's sake!*

This expression carries no literal meaning of its own, but it expresses a strong degree of exasperation.

GOOD SAMARITAN
a person who helps someone in trouble without thought of personal gain

1. Be a *good Samaritan* and volunteer some of your free time to help out at the hospital.

2. Sometimes you have to resist the urge to be a *good Samaritan* and think about your own safety. You can't pick up a strange hitchhiker in your car.

The expression has its origins in a story from the New Testament in which a man from Samaria helped someone who had been robbed by thieves.

GRASP AT STRAWS
to act in desperation with little hope of success

1. Henry tried everything he could think of to change Martha's mind, even tried things that he knew wouldn't work. He knew he was *grasping at straws*.

2. The thief told the judge one excuse after another. It was obvious that he was desperate and *grasping at straws*.

The expression suggests that whereas grasping a rope might succeed in saving one's life, *grasping at straws* (grass) is a desperate and probably useless attempt to hold on.

GRAVY TRAIN
an effortless time or job; a life of luxury

1. Scott got himself a job where he won't have to work very hard. He's really riding the *gravy train*.

2. They made some very wise and profitable investments, and now they can retire and live off the interest. They're on the *gravy train*.

GRAY MATTER
brain tissue and, by extension, intelligence

1. Anyone can see that his idea won't work. Doesn't he have any *gray matter* upstairs?

2. When it comes to *gray matter,* David got more than his fair share. He is clearly the smartest student in the class.

The expression refers to brain tissue, and suggests that one's intelligence is in direct proportion to size of one's brain.

GREEN AROUND THE GILLS
sick to one's stomach; nauseated

1. The sight of blood always makes me *green around the gills*. I always get sick to my stomach.

2. How can you eat uncooked meat? Doesn't that make you *green around the gills*?

GREEN THUMB
natural ability to grow plants

1. Amy really has a *green thumb*. Everything she plants in her garden grows so well.

2. You must have quite *a green thumb*. Your flowers are always so beautiful and healthy-looking.

The expression suggests that success with growing plants is a result of having a thumb that is the color of healthy plants.

GRIM REAPER
death

1. We'll all die in the end. You can't cheat *the grim reaper*.

2. Their grandmother was a very superstitious person and relied heavily on her intuition. She was convinced that she was about to die because she felt the *grim reaper* breathing down her neck.

The expression originates from the literary depiction of death as a hooded grim figure carrying a scythe (a farm tool made with a long, curved blade attached at an angle to a long handle). He uses the scythe to 'reap' people.

GRIN AND BEAR IT
to accept or endure a bad situation

1. Steve doesn't particularly like his job, but he's going to have to *grin and bear* it until he can find a new one.

2. I've had more than I can take from that idiot. I'm not going to *grin and bear* it for one more minute.

Compare to: *bite the bullet*

Grin and bear it literally means to smile and endure something.

HAIR'S BREADTH
a very narrow amount

1. The cars turned suddenly to avoid a collision. They missed each other by *a hair's breadth*.

2. Bill came so close to the edge that he was only *a hair's breadth* away from falling over the cliff.

Synonym: *by the skin of (one's) teeth, close shave*

The expression literally means that the distance between two things is only as great as a hair is broad.

HALF A MIND TO DO (SOMETHING)
inclined or disposed to do something; to have almost decided to do something

1. Beth has been so cold and rude to me lately, I have *half a mind not to* invite her to my party.

2. Roger was tired of his job and frequently threatened to leave the company. He had *half a mind to* quit, sell his house, and sail to Europe.

The expression is usually used to describe a threat that is not likely to be carried out.

HALF-BAKED
poorly planned or thought out

1. John suggested some *half-baked* idea to get rich quick. Anyone with any brains could see that it wouldn't work.

2. You come in here and present some *half-baked* plan to reorganize the company and fire half of the employees. That won t go over too well with the workers!

The expression suggests that when something is only *half-baked*, it is not completely cooked, i.e., not properly prepared.

HALF THE BATTLE
half the work or effort

1. Once you narrow down the topic for your dissertation, that's *half the battle*. Doing the research and writing it is the other half.

2. I finally bought all the materials to build those bookshelves. That's *half the battle*.

The expression is used to describe what may seem to be less than half the effort, a small part of the effort or just the beginning of the effort, but which in fact goes a long way to getting the work done.

HAND IN GLOVE
close or intimate

1. Tom and Kate were made for each other. They go *hand in glove*.

2. Those two workhorses pull that plow as though they were one animal. They work together *hand in glove*.

The expression refers to two people or things being as close to each other as the good fit of a hand in a glove.

HAND OVER FIST
extremely quickly

1. In the ten years we owned that house, we were never able to get it into good repair. We poured money into it *hand over fist*, but nothing helped.

2. Paul's candy was such a success at the fair, his stall was always busy with buyers. He was taking in money *hand over fist*, faster than he could count it.

The expression is usually used with money. It suggests that one draws in a fist full of money while the other hand is being extended to gather in more money in a continuous motion.

HAND TO MOUTH
to live in poor conditions from day to day; to be impoverished

1. When Brad lost his regular job, he had to take any temporary one that came along, and he never knew when he'd find another. He lived *hand to mouth*.

2. Some people in areas affected by drought live a *hand-to-mouth* existence. They collect what little food they can and never have enough to save some for another day.

The expression suggests that a person's need is so immediate that what he collects in hand goes straight into his mouth and that there is no room for saving or planning ahead.

HANDLE/TREAT (SOMEONE) WITH KID GLOVES
to treat someone cautiously or gently because he or she is easily hurt or angered

1. The boss is a difficult person to persuade—you have to approach her very carefully and put your ideas forward in just the right way. She has to be *handled with kid gloves*.

2. You can come right out and tell me what the problem is. There's no need to *handle me with kid gloves*.

The expression literally means to handle someone with gloves made of very soft kid (young goat) leather.

HANG-UP
an obsession, problem, or concern about something

1. Alan refused to let Jan pay for her movie ticket, even though the two were not on a date. Alan has a *hang-up* about what is socially acceptable and who should pay.

2. Please don t use that kind of language or tell that kind of joke around me. I'm old-fashioned, and I guess I have a *hang-up* about such crude behavior, especially in mixed company.

The expression is used to describe an obsession or concern that may be regarded as somewhat eccentric, unreasonable or illogical.

HANKY PANKY

sexual misconduct (sentence 1); mischievous behavior or activity (sentence 2); or suspicious activity (sentence 3)

1. The woman knew that her husband sometimes met with friends, both male and female, from before they were married, but she felt confident that there was no *hanky panky* going on with any of the women.

2. The children's mother thought that the children were just a little too quiet. She thought they must be up to some *hanky panky*.

3. The manager in charge of the warehouse suspected that someone was stealing some of the equipment stored there. There was definitely some *hanky panky* going on.

Synonym: *monkey business*

HAPPY-GO-LUCKY

carefree

1. Nothing depresses Charlie—he always sees the bright side of life. He's really a *happy-go-lucky* guy.

2. Sometimes sad events happen, and you just have to learn to deal with them along with the good times. Life can't always be *happy-go-lucky*.

HARD ACT TO FOLLOW

a person or thing that is so good that the person or thing that follows may not measure up to the same standard

1. The last manager of this department was hard-working and well-liked by everyone. I doubt anyone else will be as good as she was—she will be a *hard act to follow*.

2. My job here is fun, stimulating, and the pay is good. If I ever leave, it will be a *hard act to follow*.

The expression probably originates from the time of vaudeville when a show consisted of several acts, each by different actors. It was hard to succeed if one's act followed another that was extremely popular, because the audience would compare the two and expect the second act to measure up to the high standard of the first.

HARD/TOUGH ROW TO HOE

a difficult task

1. Going to medical school is not going to be easy. In fact, it will be a *tough row to hoe*.

2. Life can be a *hard row to hoe*. You have to put a roof over your head and food on the table, and it's not easy for anyone.

The expression suggests that using a hoe (a garden tool) to weed a row of plants can sometimes be a difficult task.

HAVE/GOT IT MADE

to have no problems; to have achieved success

1. Elaine has a great job, a nice home, and a good family. She doesn't need anything else; I think she's really *got it made*.

2. Remember Larry, the artist? He married a wealthy woman and now he doesn't have to do odd jobs to support himself anymore. He *has it made*.

HAVE THE LAST LAUGH

to outsmart or get revenge on someone who thinks he or she has been clever

1. The boys thought they had tricked the girls by locking them in the kitchen, but he girls *had the last laugh* when the boys got hungry and realized they couldn t get in.

2. Mark was lazy and decided to let Roger do most of the work. But Roger *had the last laugh* because, in the end, Mark got none of the credit.

Compare to: *he who laughs last, laughs best; laugh all the way to the bank*

HEAD AND SHOULDERS ABOVE

at a much higher level

1. Lisa's work is outstanding and no one's comes close to being so good. Her work is *head and shoulders above* everyone else's.

2. This performance of the play was *head and shoulders above* the previous performance. The actors really did an excellent job this time.

Compare to: *run circles around (someone); not hold a candle to (something)*

The expression suggests that someone or something that is *head and shoulders above* someone or something else is substantially better. Whereas run circles around someone means to outperform someone (usually physically), *head and shoulders above someone* usually refers to a person's or object's character or inner qualities.

HEAD HONCHO

a person with power in a company or organization

1. If you want to spend that kind of money on your project, you'll probably have to get permission from the *head honchos*. If I were you, I'd make an appointment with your boss.

2. The director wanted to include a big battle scene in his movie, but the *head honchos* at the studio wouldn't allow it.

HEAD IN THE CLOUDS, HAVE (ONE'S)

to be impractical or absent-minded; to be unaware of what is going on around one

1. I don't know where my mind is today—I can't keep my thoughts on my work. My *head is in the clouds*.

2. Don't go to Susan for advice; she'll give you some romantic and impractical solution to your love life. She always has her *head in the clouds*.

Antonyms: *down to earth; both feet on the ground*

The expression suggests that one whose head is in the clouds is out of touch with the reality around him/her.

HEAD OVER HEELS IN LOVE

very much in love; uncontrollably in love

1. Richard fell in love with Pamela the first time he saw her, and now he can't think about anything else. He is *head over heels in love* with her.

2. In the 1960s, many young girls in the United States and Europe fell *head over heels in love* with the pop singers the Beatles.

HEAR (SOMETHING) THROUGH THE GRAPEVINE

to hear a rumor that may or may not be true

1. No one knows it yet, but I found out that the boss is about to quit. I can't tell you who told me, but let's just say I *heard it though the grapevine*.

2. "How did you find out Karen was going to have a baby?" I asked. "I *heard it through the grapevine*," answered Julie.

Antonym: *straight from the horse's mouth*

The expression suggests that a grapevine, long, tangled and indirect, can act as a means of communication, but the message is not direct and may be distorted or untrue.

HEART TO HEART

serious and intimate

1. I have to talk to you about something that is serious and very important to both of us. I want to have a *heart-to-heart* talk with you.

2. You always make a joke about everything, and you never talk to me seriously about things that are important. Don't you ever talk *heart to heart* with anyone?

The expression is usually used to describe an important and sincere talk between two people.

HEAVYWEIGHT

a person who is important and influential; a leader in a particular field

1. The two important and well-known authors John Steinbeck and Ernest Hemingway are *heavyweights* in American literature.

2. You cannot dismiss the importance and influence of *heavyweight* Steven Spielberg on the movie industry. His use of high-tech visual effects has become the new standard for action films.

Synonyms: *bigwig; force to be reckoned with*

Antonym: *lightweight*

The expression suggests that the person carries a lot of weight and therefore influence in a particular field. A *bigwig* is frequently limited to the business world and suggests a person who is high up on the corporate ladder. *A force to be reckoned with* can be used to describe someone or something that is powerful, and may instill a sense of fear that *heavyweight* does not. The expressions *heavyweight* and *lightweight* come from the sport of boxing. Boxers are put into classes according to their weights. *Heavyweight* is the heaviest class, with boxers weighing more than 175 pounds or 81 kilograms.

HELL TO PAY, HAVE

(to be) in serious trouble

1. I don't know how the accident happened, but the car fender is ruined. I'm going to have *hell to pay* when I get home.

2. Your parents told you not to be late getting home again. If you don't get home on time tonight, you'll have *hell to pay*.

Synonyms: *in Dutch; in hot water; in the doghouse*

HEM AND HAW

to hesitate to say something directly

1. Andrew wanted to ask Gail to marry him but he couldn t find the words. He stood there, hat in hand, *hemming and hawing*.

2. You don't have to be afraid to tell me what happened. Stop *hemming and hawing* and get to the point.

Compare to: *beat around the bush; stonewall*

The expression probably originates from the sounds one might make when clearing one's throat and trying to introduce a delicate subject.

HIT OR MISS

unplanned or random; equally likely to succeed or fail

1. Sometimes Ann is at home when I drop by to visit her, and sometimes she's not. It's *hit or miss* catching her at home.

2. The repairman's work is *hit or miss*. Sometimes the machine works when he's finished fixing it, and sometimes it doesn't.

HIT PAY DIRT

to find something of great value

1. They invested their money in oil wells in Texas and they *hit pay dirt*. Now they're the richest people I know.

2. Chuck went off to Alaska looking to *hit pay dirt*, but I don't think he's going to find what he wants. Everything worth finding has already been claimed.

3. The senator's enemies started to investigate his past in the hopes of finding something scandalous. They *hit pay dirt* when they uncovered his driving record and found that he had been arrested for drunk driving.

Synonym: *strike it rich*

Compare to: *hit the jackpot*

The expression originates from the mining and gold-rush days when a person could become rich if he or she found dirt with gold in it.

HIT THE JACKPOT
to get rich or find something of value

1. Mabel always bought one lottery ticket in the hopes that one day she would *hit the jackpot* and never have to work again.

2. I went to the library not expecting to find any of the books that were on my list, but I *hit the jackpot*. I managed to find all seven of them.

Synonym: *hit pay dirt*

The expression originates from gambling, in which the jackpot is the money collected from the gamblers and divided among the winners.

HIT THE NAIL ON THE HEAD
to come to the right conclusion

1. Henry wouldn't tell his wife what was wrong, but when she asked him if he had lost his job, she could tell by the look on his face that she had *hit the nail on the head*.

2. We sat around the table trying to figure out why the project wasn't working. Everyone suggested ideas and possibilities. When Leslie outlined what she thought the problem was, we could all see that she had *hit the nail on the head*.

Synonym: *put (one's) finger on it/(something), get (something) on the nose*

HIT THE SACK
to go to bed

1. I'm really tired—I can t keep my eyes open any longer. I'm going to *hit the sack*.

2. After a hard day, Richard decided to *hit the sack* even though it was only 8:00 p.m.

HIT THE SPOT
to satisfy in just the right way

1. The boys were sweating from planting trees in the hot sun. When their mother brought them some cold lemonade to drink, it really *hit the spot*.

2. I think I'd like something to eat after the theater. A little light supper after the play will just *hit the spot*.

Compare to: *fill/fit the bill*

The expression is often used in reference to food or drink.

HITCH/THUMB A RIDE
to solicit a ride in someone's (a stranger's) car; to hitchhike

1. Julian had no car, but he needed to visit his mother in the hospital in another town, so he *hitched a ride*.

2. The boys had no way to get to the beach, about 60 miles away. They decided to stand by the side of the highway and *thumb a ride*.

The expression *thumb a ride* denotes that the traveler solicits the ride by standing on the side of the road and extending his or her thumb toward passing cars.

HOLD A CANDLE TO (SOMEONE), NOT
not equal to someone or something; when two persons or things are compared, the first one is clearly inferior to the second one

1. This house *doesn't hold a candle to the one* we looked at yesterday. The one we saw yesterday was practically twice the size and had much better light.

2. Marjorie's cakes *can't hold a candle to* Kate's. Kate's are light, fluffy and flavorful, and Marjorie's are as heavy as lead.

Compare to: *head and shoulders above (someone); run circles around (someone)*

HOLD (ONE'S) BREATH, NOT
to not wait for something to happen because it probably won't happen soon, if at all

1. Shirley said she would come, but *don't hold your breath*. She often doesn't show up, even when she says she will.

2. I'm hoping they will decide to buy the house, but I'm *not holding my breath*. So many things can go wrong with the deal.

The expression is always used in the negative.

HOLD (ONE'S) HORSES
to stay calm or be patient when someone wants to hurry

1. The children were ready to go, but their father was not. They kept bothering him until he told them to *hold their horses*.

2. Now just *hold your horses*. I know you're in a hurry, but you can't go outside without your coat on in this chilly weather.

Synonym: *keep (one's) shirt on*

Antonyms: *shake a leg; step on it*

The expression is generally used in the imperative. It is used by an adult to children, a superior to an inferior or between two equals on friendly or intimate terms.

HOLD (ONE'S) OWN
to be able to withstand opposition or attack; to do just as well as other people

1. Sarah may be the smallest child in the class, but when it comes to defending herself, she can *hold her own*.

2. We didn t think Mark was very good at speaking, but he really *held his own* in that debate.

HOLD (ONE'S) TONGUE
to refrain from speaking

1. Ella wanted to talk to Bob immediately, but there were too many people around, so she *held her tongue* and waited until they were alone.

2. The young boy began shouting at his mother, and she lost her temper and told him to *hold his tongue.* She told him it was not polite to talk to anyone like that.

3. I've listened to you criticizing him and I've *held my tongue,* but I can't any longer. Now I'm going to tell you some of the positive sides of his character.

HOLD (SOMEONE/SOMETHING) AT BAY
to prevent someone or something that is threatening or attacking from being able to advance

1. The hen *held the dog at bay* while her baby chicks ran for safety.

2. They *held the soldiers at bay* with their swords for as long as they could, but in the end, they were defeated.

HOLD THE FORT
to take care of a place or to keep an activity going while someone is away

1. The manager left the store to go to lunch. She asked the sales clerk to *hold the fort* while she was gone.

2. I got the party started and then discovered that I had to leave to get some more food. I asked my friend to *hold the fort* until I got back.

The expression probably originates from the idea of defending (holding) a fort under attack.

HOLD WATER
to be credible or sound; to stand up to scrutiny; to make sense

1. The politician argued that they had to raise taxes, but the reasons he gave didn't *hold water.*

2. Two scientists claimed that they had achieved fusion at room temperature. Other scientists wanted to test the theory to see if it would *hold water.*

The expression is used in reference to arguments or ideas rather than people.

HOOK, LINE, AND SINKER, FALL FOR/ SWALLOW (SOMETHING)
to believe something completely, usually in the sense of being fooled

1. The children made up such a believable story that their mother *fell for it hook, line and sinker.*

2. The salesman was such a smooth talker, he could make anyone believe his stories. People always *swallowed them hook, line and sinker.*

The expression originates from fishing. One expects the fish to bite only the hook, but in some cases the fish might be taken in so completely and foolishly that it swallows not only the hook but the fishing line and the sinker as well.

HOOKED
addicted

1. When he started smoking, Keith didn't believe that the nicotine in cigarettes was addictive, but now he is *hooked* on it.

2. I love reading detective stories, and I read at least two every week. I'm *hooked* on them.

The expression can refer to a physical addiction (sentence 1) or it can have the sense of being very enthusiastic about something (sentence 2).

HOPPING MAD
very angry

When Bill found out that Sandra had blamed her mistake on him, he was *hopping mad* and threatened to tell their boss about all of the things she had done wrong.

The basketball player was *hopping mad* when the referee didn't call the other team's foul, but he knew that getting angry would only get him ejected from the game.

HORSE AROUND
to play a little roughly

1. Don't forget we're in a library, boys. People are trying to read quietly and concentrate on their work. *Stop horsing around.*

2. The children should not *horse around* in the garage. There are too many dangerous tools in there.

Synonyms: *clown around; monkey around; fool around*

Horse around emphasizes the physical nature of the play whereas *clown around* means to act silly, and *monkey around* means to fiddle or tinker with something.

HORSE OF ANOTHER COLOR
a situation or plan which represents a change from what was expected or assumed

1. Yesterday you said you wanted to go to the movies with a friend, and I assumed you meant a girlfriend. If you want to go with Ken, that's a *horse of another color.*

2. At first, the unions accepted management's offer of a 10% pay raise until they realized that management meant to spread the raise over four years instead of over two. To the unions, that was a *horse of another color.*

HORSE SENSE
common sense (sentence 1) or shrewdness; cleverness (sentence 2)

1. You just don't have any *horse sense* when it comes to looking after yourself. You stay up late, don't get enough sleep and eat poorly.

2. I took my father along when I went to shop for a new car. He has real *horse sense* and can spot a good deal.

The expression probably originates from the idea that a person who knew what to look for in a horse (i.e., had a sense for horses) could find the best horses to buy.

HOT UNDER THE COLLAR
very angry

1. When Tammy tried to blame the mistake on Sue, Sue *got hot under the collar.*

2. I *get hot under the collar* every time I remember how rude the bank manager was to us.

Antonym: *keep (one's) cool*

Compare to: *lose (one's) temper; make (someone's) blood boil*

HUFF AND PUFF
to be out of breath (sentence 1) or to threaten ineffectually (sentence 2)

1. All the runners were out of breath and were *huffing and puffing* by the end of the marathon.

2. Mrs. Rene returned to the shop to complain about the service she had gotten from a new sales clerk. After she left, the manager told the sales clerk not to be too concerned. "Mrs. Rene is always *huffing and puffing* about something or other. She doesn't really mean anything by it," said the manager.

A *huff* is a feeling of displeasure or resentment. A *puff* is a burst of breath.

I

IF/WHEN PUSH COMES TO SHOVE
if the situation becomes serious

1. The president isn't a forceful woman, but *if push comes to shove,* she stands firm and lets her feelings be known.

2. I thought my parents wouldn't support my beliefs because mine were different from theirs, but *when push came to shove,* they were right there in my corner fighting for me.

IN A BIND/FIX/JAM
in a difficult situation or position

1. Can I borrow $10 from you? *I'm in a bind.* The banks have closed and I need to stop at the supermarket on the way home.

2. Sam is really *in a fix.* He accepted a job last Friday that he doesn't particularly want because he didn't think he would get a better offer. Now he has been offered a job he wants, but he doesn't know how to get out of the first job.

3. I'm *in a jam.* I have a doctor's appointment at the same time as I have to pick the children up from school. Do you think you could get the children for me?

Synonyms: *over a barrel; between the devil and the deep blue sea; between a rock and a hard place*

In a bind is less dramatic than these last two expressions, which would be used when a problem has no apparent solution. *Between the devil and the deep blue sea* and *between a rock and a hard place* would not be appropriate in the situations presented in sentences 1 or 3, for example.

IN A NUTSHELL
concisely; in a few words

1. You can't go to the movies tonight because tomorrow is a school day, you're supposed to be saving your money, and you just went to the movies last night. Now, if you want it *in a nutshell,* the answer is no.

2. We're eager to find out what her plans are. Tell us *in a nutshell*: is she going or not?

Compare to: *long and short of it; nitty gritty; bottom line*

The expression suggests that the words are so few that they can fit in a nutshell.

IN A PINCH
in an emergency; if necessary

1. My car has only six seats but it can carry eight people *in a pinch.*

2. We would prefer one large double room at the hotel, but two small ones will be all right *in a pinch.*

IN A RUT
in a boring routine

1. I'm tired of this job. I do the same old thing day in and day out. I'm *in a rut.*

2. Don't let yourself get *into a rut.* Try something new from time to time, and you won't get bored.

Synonym: *on a treadmill*

Compare to: *old hat*

A *rut* is a groove or narrow track pressed into a dirt road that catches the wheel of a vehicle and forces the vehicle to go in a restricted path that the driver is unable to alter. The expression connotes going in a direction or doing an activity without being able to vary it.

IN BLACK AND WHITE
in print or in writing

1. You can't agree to buy or sell a house with just a handshake. The agreement has to be *in black and white.*

2. I didn't believe what you were telling me was true, but here it is in the newspaper *in black and white.*

The expression originates from the black and white colors of ink on paper.

IN DUTCH (WITH)
in trouble

1. My parents said I'd better get home on time or I'll be *in Dutch.*

2. The boys got *in Dutch with* the teacher when they didn't turn in their homework.

Synonym: *in hot water, in the doghouse, hell to pay*

In the doghouse is less serious and often light-hearted. To have *hell to pay* is generally stronger and more serious.

IN FULL SWING
at the peak of activity or intensity

1. Julie arrived about 30 minutes late and the party was already *in full swing.*

2. The meeting started at 4:00 p.m. It was still *in full swing* when the assistant manager arrived a little after 6:00.

IN HOT WATER
in trouble

1. Cheryl borrowed her mother's best silk blouse without permission and spilled soda on it. She knew she'd be *in hot water* when she got home.

2. I got *in hot water* with my parents because I failed mathematics.

Synonym: *in Dutch, all hell to pay; in the doghouse*

IN/OUT OF (ONE'S) ELEMENT
in one's most comfortable or favorite environment

1. Diana is *in her element* when she's in the classroom. She's a natural teacher.

2. I love being in the country. When I'm in the city, I'm lost. I'm *out of my element*.

Compare to: *out of (one's) depth; fish out of water; in (way) over one's head*

Out of one's element describes being uncomfortable in an environment, whereas *out of one's depth* describes being asked to perform beyond one's capability.

IN OVER (ONE'S) HEAD
beyond one's capability (sentence 1); to have taken on more than one can cope with (sentence 2)

1. Tim can't compete with these people. They are much more capable in their field than he is. He's *in way over his head.*

2. Be careful how much work you take on. Don't promise to do more than you can handle. Don't get *in over your head.*

Synonyms: *out of (one's) depth/league* (sentence 1); *bite off more than (one) can chew* (sentence 2)

IN STITCHES, HAVE (SOMEONE)/BE IN)
to make someone laugh very hard

1. We hired a very funny clown to perform at the company picnic. He had the children *in stitches* from beginning to end.

2. The movie was hilarious. We couldn t stop laughing. We *were in stitches.*

IN THE BAG
a sure thing; success is assured

1. The personnel director said that I was the best candidate for the job and that if I pass the typing test tomorrow, the job is *in the bag.*

2. I know you think the scholarship is *in the bag,* but don t get your hopes up too high.

IN THE BLACK
making a profit

1. The company lost money the first four years but now it's making money and is finally *in the black.*

2. The government hasn t been *in the black* for the last 20 years. It has been spending more money than it brings in through taxes.

3. Although we aren't losing money, we're not *in the black* either. We're just breaking even.

Antonym: *in the red*

The expression originates from the color of ink that was used on the credit side of a business ledger or account book.

IN THE CHIPS/MONEY
having lots of money

1. I would quit work and spend the rest of my life travelling around the world if I were *in the chips.*

2. You children are asking for so many Christmas presents, you'd think I was *in the money.*

The expression originates from a game like poker in which chips represent money.

IN THE DOGHOUSE
in someone's bad graces; in trouble

1. Frank looked at his watch and realized that he was over an hour late for an appointment with his wife. "I'm really going to be *in the doghouse* this time," he said.

2. Dianne used her mother's car without permission and now she's *in the doghouse.*

Compare to: *in Dutch; in hot water; all hell to pay*

Usually the "someone" in the expression is a loved one and the situation or trouble is not very serious. *In Dutch* and *in hot water* are more serious, and *(have) all hell to pay* is generally much stronger and more serious.

IN THE LONG RUN
in the end; after a long time has passed (sentence 1); after weighing all the advantages and disadvantages (sentence 2)

1. Jenny couldn t decide whether to study accounting or law at college. She didn't know which major she would be happier with *in the long run*. She might grow to dislike one or the other in 20 years.

2. Brian had his own car, but he chose to take the train to work every day even though it took more time. It was easier *in the long run* because he didn't have to tolerate traffic jams, pay for gas, or look for parking.

IN THE LOOP
informed

Sharon had worked with the same team for nearly two years, but she still didn't feel like she was *in the loop*. She still had to ask for information from her colleagues.

I'd be happy to let you work on that project by yourself, but I'd like to know how you're progressing. Remember to keep me *in the loop*, please.

IN THE NICK OF TIME
at the last moment, just before something bad happens

1. The accident victim was near death, but the ambulance arrived *in the nick of time* and the paramedic saved her.

2. We ran as fast as we could toward the bus stop and got there just as the bus was pulling to a stop. We got there *in the nick of time.*

Compare to: *down to the wire; under the wire.*

IN THE PINK
in good health or good condition

1. After several days in the hospital, Paul wanted to go home. He told the doctor he was feeling *in the pink* and there was no reason for him to stay any longer.

2. I always get my car serviced on time. That way it stays in the *pink* and I don't have to worry about it breaking down.

Antonym: *under the weather*

In the pink can be applied to both people and things, while *under the weather* is limited to people. The expression probably originates from the idea that a healthy person's complexion is described as pink, while a sick person's skin is pale or chalky.

IN THE RED
losing money; not making a profit

1. Many governments operate year after year *in the red*. They simply keep borrowing money against the taxes they expect to collect in the future.

2. Some years my business makes a profit, but other years I'm *in the red*.

Antonym: *in the black*

The expression originates from the color of ink that was used on the debit (loss) side of a business ledger or account book.

IN THE SAME BOAT
in the same bad situation

1. Jake and I both lost our jobs yesterday. Now we're *in the same boat*.

2. Our landlord raised the rent on our apartments, and none of us can afford to stay here any longer. We're all *in the same boat*.

The expression suggests that people in the same boat share the same bad fate. They will all sink together if the boat capsizes.

IN/OUT OF THE MAINSTREAM
in the group that represents the majority; *out of the mainstream* means on the edge of the majority

1. Andy Warhol was a painter whose work is representative of the Pop Art period. He was *in the mainstream* of Pop Art painting.

2. That politician advocates very extreme views that are entirely different from most of the other politicians. He is *out of the mainstream* of current politics.

IT'S ALL GREEK TO ME
incomprehensible or unintelligible

1. I'm not very good at understanding the directions on how to assemble these modern-day toys. They're *all Greek to me*.

2. Can you tell me what this page says? I don't even know if it's right side up or upside down. *It's all Greek to me.*

The expression can be traced back as far as Shakespeare's play *Julius Caesar*, and probably originates from the idea that the Greek language uses a different alphabet from English, making it difficult for English speakers to hear or understand.

IT'S NO SKIN OFF (SOMEONE'S) NOSE
it has no effect on someone or it is of no concern to someone

1. I think you're crazy to spend your money on that car, but it's your decision. It's no *skin off my nose*.

2. Don't tell me what to do with my life. It's no *skin off your nose* if I choose to quit school.

IVORY TOWER
an isolated environment where one is out of touch with everyday reality; a place of retreat where one concentrates on intellectual rather than everyday matters

1. The boss felt that he couldn't consider Richard for the difficult job of manager because Richard seemed out of touch with the workers. He was isolated in his *ivory tower*.

2. When the professors complained that the students couldn t meet the academic standards of the past, they were told that they should come out of their *ivory tower*. More students attend the university now and it can't be as selective as it used to be.

The expression suggests an ivory (white) tower high above the masses. An *ivory tower* is often associated with an academic or university environment, which is said to be isolated from the real world, e.g., business and politics.

J

JACK OF ALL TRADES

a person who knows a little about a lot of different subjects or activities, but not a lot about any one of them

1. Walt is good at so many things: he can fix the plumbing and wiring in his house, he fixed his roof when it leaked, he installed his washer and dryer, and he paints the house when it needs it. He's really *a jack of all trades.*

2. The position in the company required someone who knew everything about a very narrow subject. They weren't looking for *a jack of all trades.*

The expression is part of the saying "He's *a jack of all trades* but a master of none." Being described as a *jack of all trades* can be either a compliment (usually when it is used without the second half of the saying) or an insult (when it occurs in the saying and the emphasis is on the fact that one is master of none).

JOHN HANCOCK

one's signature

1. If you'll just put your *John Hancock* on this line at the bottom of the contract, you can drive the car away right now.

2. They sent the check back because he forgot to put his *John Hancock* on it.

The expression refers to the signature of the first person to sign the American Declaration of Independence in 1776. *John Hancock's* signature was larger than the others and stood out clearly.

JOHNNY-COME-LATELY

a newcomer

1. You can't expect to join the company, take over immediately, and not cause some hard feelings. To the workers, you're *a Johnny-come-lately.*

2. The author of the book was under attack because he was *a Johnny-come-lately* to the field and didn't have the reputation that the older, more established authors had.

Compare to: *wet behind the ears*

The expression is used to dismiss someone's importance due to a lack of experience.

JUMP THE GUN

to do something prematurely; to start early, before all the preparations have been made.

1. You can't begin the project yet. You're going to have to wait until the plan is thoroughly developed. Don't *jump the gun.*

2. *You* bought your son a football and he's only six weeks old. Don't you think you're *jumping the gun* a little?

The expression probably originates from foot racing, in which an overly anxious runner would accidentally begin the race before the starting gun was fired.

JUMPING-OFF POINT

a starting place or inspiration

1. Kelly used her mother's lasagna recipe as a *jumping-off point*, but added her favorite ingredients to make it the way she liked it.

2. Joe used sheet music as a *jumping-off point* for his song. He played the tune as written, but added to it as he went.

This expression is usually used for discussions or creative pursuits.

JUNK FOOD

food that is relatively unhealthy, high in sugar and fat and lacking in vitamins, minerals and other body-building components

1. My children seem to live on *junk food:* hamburgers, French fries, milkshakes, chips, cakes, cookies, candy, and soda pop.

2. The parents brought snacks for the children to eat. The school had asked them to bring healthy foods like fresh fruit and vegetables, yogurt and cheese. They asked them not to bring *junk food.*

K

KANGAROO COURT

a court set up outside the regular legal system; staged trial where the outcome is set from the beginning

1. The rancher and his friends tried and convicted the horse thieves in a *kangaroo court* rather than let the sheriff take them to jail for a trial according to the law.

2. The political protesters had been tried and found guilty in a court of law, and when the verdict was read, they claimed that the jury and judge had not been impartial, and that they had been tried in a *kangaroo court*.

KEEP (ONE'S) COOL

to stay calm under stress; not to become angry

1. I know you're angry, but you've got to try to control yourself. *Keep your cool* and don't lose your temper.

2. It's particularly important to *keep your cool* in a traffic jam. It's so easy to get angry and have an accident.

Synonym: *hold/lose (one's) temper*

Antonym: *lose (one's) cool, hot under the collar; see red*

KEEP (ONE'S) EYES PEELED

to be alert and watchful; to look very carefully for something or someone

1. I'm looking for a special edition of a book, and I haven't found it anywhere. When you're in the bookstore, please *keep your eyes peeled* for it, will you?

2. They planned to meet Joe on a crowded corner at lunchtime. He hadn't arrived yet, but as people walked toward the corner, they *kept their eyes peeled* for him.

The expression suggests that one's eyelids are pulled back in order to not miss seeing anything.

KEEP (ONE'S) FINGERS CROSSED

to hope for something; to wish for luck

1. Jane wasn't sure that she had passed the test, but she was *keeping her fingers crossed*.

2. They are *keeping their fingers crossed* that the rain holds off and doesn't spoil the picnic they have planned.

The expression probably originates from a superstition that bad luck can be prevented by crossing one's fingers. The expression refers to crossing one's middle finger over the knuckle of the index finger.

KEEP (ONE'S) HEAD ABOVE WATER

to just barely manage to stay ahead, financially (sentence 1) or with one's work or responsibilities (sentence 2)

1. Mrs. Robinson has three children to support and she doesn't make very much money at her job. She is barely *keeping her head above water*.

2. Peter is having a difficult time at the university because he wasn't very well prepared academically, but he is somehow managing to *keep his head above water*.

Antonym: *in over (one's) head*

Compare to: *make ends meet; get by*

Keep one's head above water and *make ends meet* mean having just enough money but no extra, although the former conveys a greater feeling of desperation. *Keep one's head above water* can mean survival in a financial or other sense, whereas *make ends meet* always refers to a financial situation.

KEEP (ONE'S) NOSE TO THE GRINDSTONE

to work hard without rest

1. You will succeed if you keep working hard, but you have to *keep your nose to the grindstone*.

2. Kim is studying constantly now because she has final exams next week. She's in her room *keeping her nose to the grindstone*.

The expression usually refers to monotonous work.

KEEP (ONE'S) SHIRT ON

to stay calm or be patient when someone wants to hurry

1. Will you *keep your shirt on*, Bob? You won't get there any faster if you drive too fast and cause a car accident.

2. I know you're hungry, but dinner won't be ready for another ten minutes. Just *keep your shirt on!*

Synonym: *hold (one's) horses*

Antonyms: *shake a leg; step on it*

The expression is generally used in the imperative. It is used by an adult to children, a superior to a subordinate, or between two equals on friendly or intimate terms.

KEEP (ONE'S) WITS ABOUT (ONE)

to pay attention and be ready to react

1. If she wants to do well in her job interview, she can t daydream—she'll have to *keep her wits about her*.

2. When I travel, I'm always careful to keep my things with me in crowded places. I *keep my wits about me*.

Compare to: *at (one's) wits' end, scared out of (one's) wits*

KEEP (SOMEONE) AT ARM'S LENGTH
to keep someone at a distance emotionally

1. You can't expect people to be very friendly to you when you always *keep them at arm's length*.

2. Craig thinks that if he *keeps everyone at arm's length*, he won't fall in love and get hurt.

KEEP (SOMETHING) UNDER (ONE'S) HAT
to keep something secret

1. Don't tell Richard anything you don't want everyone else to know. It's impossible for him to *keep anything under his hat*.

2. I'm not telling anyone yet, but Tom and I are getting married. *Keep it under your hat,* okay?

Antonyms: *spill the beans; let the cat out of the bag*

This phrase originates from the 1800s, when many men and women wore hats. The idea is to keep a secret in your head, underneath a hat.

KEEP THE BALL ROLLING
to maintain momentum; to keep some process going

1. The principal has done so much and worked so hard to improve this school. Who's going to *keep the ball rolling* when she retires?

2. Mr. Preston had managed to motivate his employees to higher production levels, and he wanted to keep them going. He wondered how he could *keep the ball rolling*.

KEEP UP WITH THE JONESES
to have the same standard of living as one's friends and neighbors do

1. My wife seems to think that we should buy our children cars of their own just because most of our friends do. She seems to think we have to *keep up with the Joneses*.

2. *Keeping up with the Joneses* can be very expensive. Every time your neighbor improves his home or buys a new car, you feel you have to, too.

The expression implies that one strains one's financial resources when one tries to match or exceed the purchases or actions made by a neighbor.

Jones is a common family name.

KEYED UP
full of nervous anticipation; anxious; tense

1. Stop pacing the floor. Relax. Why are you *so keyed up?*

2. Charles was *so keyed up* waiting for the wedding to begin that when it finally did, he dropped the wedding ring.

KICK THE BUCKET
to die

1. I plan on spending all my money before I *kick the bucket*. I'm not going to leave a penny of it to my relatives.

2. Your father hasn't yet made a will. He doesn't plan on *kicking the bucket* anytime soon.

3. The old woman was a person everyone in the neighborhood disliked. There were not too many mourners when she *kicked the bucket*.

The expression can be either disparaging or light-hearted when used about oneself or one's relatives (sentences 1 and 2), or disrespectful and impolite when used about someone else (sentence 3).

KICK UP (ONE'S) HEELS
to have a lively and fun time, usually at a party or dance

1. Mr. and Mrs. Taylor are certainly having a good time at the party. They haven't *kicked up their heels* like this for years.

2. Put down your work, get out of the house, and come to the dance. Why don't you *kick up your heels* for a change?

The expression is commonly used to describe someone who is ordinarily quiet and reserved and for whom having a lively time is unusual.

KILL TWO BIRDS WITH ONE STONE
to accomplish two objectives with one action

1. I have to go to New York on business this Friday, and I've needed to get some new suits for some time. Maybe I can *kill two birds with one stone*: I'll attend to my business in New York on Friday and Monday and do some shopping over the weekend.

2. I need to get rid of all the old baby clothes I had for my children when they were small. Since you are about to have your first baby, why don't I give the clothes to you? We'll *kill two birds with one stone*.

KNEE-HIGH TO A GRASSHOPPER
very young

1. I was just *knee-high to a grasshopper* when I first went fishing with my father. I couldn't have been more than five years old.

2. Look how small these pants are! I must have been *knee-high to a grasshopper* the last time I wore them.

The expression suggests that the person is only as tall as a grasshopper's knee and is therefore very young. It is often used with a facedown, open hand to indicate the young person's height at the time.

KNOCK/THROW (SOMEONE) FOR A LOOP [KNOCKED/THROWN FOR A LOOP]
to shock, surprise, or astound someone

1. The teacher *threw me for a loop* when she told me I had failed the exam. I thought I had done so well.

2. Alan was *knocked for a loop* when he found out he had won $5,000 in the lottery.

Compare to: *pull the rug out from under (someone); spring something on (someone)*

KNOW BEANS ABOUT SOMETHING, NOT
to know very little about something; to speak without authority on some topic

1. Rita's interpretation of that artist is completely wrong. Don't listen to her. She *doesn't know beans about it.*

2. Sometimes you go on and on as though you're an expert. I bet *you don't know* beans about half the things you think you do.

Similar to: *talk through one's hat*

KNOW IF (ONE) IS COMING OR GOING, NOT
to be confused and disoriented

1. Nancy thought yesterday was Wednesday and now she thinks today is Sunday. She *doesn't know if she's coming or going.*

2. First I packed all the wrong clothes, then left the bag behind, and waited for the taxi until I realized I had forgotten to call one. When it came, I couldn't remember where I wanted to go. I don't *know if I'm coming or going.*

Antonyms: *on the ball; get/have (one's) act together*

Compare to: *out to lunch*

KNOW (SOMEONE) FROM ADAM, NOT
to be unable to recognize someone because the person is a stranger

1. Who is that speaking at the podium? Is it the chairman? I don t *know him from Adam.*

2. A strange woman approached us at the train station. I assumed that she was Mrs. Smith, whom we were supposed to meet, but it was hard to tell since we didn't *know Mrs. Smith from Adam.*

KNOW THE INS AND OUTS
to be familiar with the details and hidden meanings of an activity or situation

1. When you travel to a foreign country, it is wise to hire a guide if you don't know the *ins and outs* of the place.

2. American businesses often hire host country nationals to help them do business in foreign countries because the host country nationals *know the ins and outs* of doing business with their own countrymen.

Compare to: *know the ropes*

Know the ropes is more frequently used to describe knowing the procedures to follow in a situation (knowing how to do something), whereas *know the ins and outs* more often describes the complex and hidden details of a situation.

KNOW THE ROPES
to be familiar with a task or situation

1. Let Marilyn help you get the manuscript published the first time. She *knows the ropes* and she'll save you a lot of time and effort.

2. You have to *know the ropes* if you want to get hired in this city. Employers are looking for people with connections and know-how, not untried youngsters fresh out of college.

Antonym: *wet behind the ears*

Compare to: *learn the ropes; know the ins and outs*

Know the ropes is more frequently used to describe knowing the procedures to follow in a given situation (how to do something), whereas *ins and outs* more often describes the complex and hidden details of a situation.

KNUCKLE DOWN
to do one's work seriously; to apply oneself fully; to get busy

1. The young man hadn't been studying very much and now he was failing his courses. The student advisor told him he would have to *knuckle down* if he wanted to avoid being expelled.

2. Mary frequently complains that she doesn't have enough time to finish her work. But if she would spend less time chatting and just *knuckle down*, she would get it done.

KNUCKLE UNDER
to submit or give in to pressure

1. Don't let society beat you down or make you be the way everyone else is. Don t *knuckle under.*

2. The mob leader promised that they would never make him reveal his partners in crime, no matter how badly they treated him. He swore he would never *knuckle under.*

Antonyms: *stand (one's) ground; stick to (one's) guns*

L

LABOR OF LOVE
something done out of affection or great interest

1. Martha loves to knit sweaters for her children. She could buy them for less money than it costs her to make them, but they are a *labor of love* for her.

2. When Ralph built a wagon for his son, he picked out the wood himself, carefully sanded each piece, and handpainted it with more coats of paint than necessary. Building the wagon was a *labor of love* because it was for his son.

LAME DUCK
a person who holds an office but has little real influence because he or she has not been reelected

1. After an election, a *lame duck* congress often gets a lot of serious work done because the members who have been voted out are no longer running for office and no longer have to worry about pleasing their constituents.

2. The board of directors chose a new chairman to take over running the company. The old chairman had a few weeks left before he had to step aside, but his workers no longer feared him because he was a *lame duck*.

The expression suggests that a lame duck—a duck that cannot fly—is ineffectual. It originally comes from the 1760s London Stock Market, where it referred to investors who were unable to pay their debts.

LAP OF LUXURY, LIVE IN THE
to be very comfortable because one is well-off financially

1. Because she was the richest movie star in the business, she had a magnificent house, servants, cars and clothes. She was *living in the lap of luxury*.

2. If this business deal succeeds, we'll never have to worry about money again. *We'll be living in the lap of luxury*.

The *lap of luxury* means a very comfortable life because one is rich, whereas the *life of Riley* is an easygoing life because one doesn't have to work or isn't working. Someone who is poor can lead the *life of Riley* if he or she doesn't mind being poor.

LAST BUT NOT LEAST
the final item on a list, but not the least important

1. If you want to borrow my car, you have to follow the rules. First, you must obey the speed limit, fill up the gas tank before you bring it back, and bring it back before I need it tomorrow. *Last but not least*, you may not drive it if you have been drinking alcohol.

2. John accomplished a lot in his lifetime. He was a teacher and an activist for the poor, he wrote several books, and *last but not least*, he raised four successful children.

The expression is used before the last in a series of items to indicate that it is not less important for being last. Usually the series has been randomly arranged and no specific order of importance has been assigned to the items.

LAST-DITCH EFFORT
a very strenuous final attempt

1. I'm going to try a *last-ditch effort* to uproot this old oak tree myself before I call the tree company to come and do it by machine.

2. Ronnie slipped and fell as he ran to catch the baseball, but when he looked up, the ball was still sailing through the air. Ronnie got up and made a *last-ditch effort* to catch the ball.

The expression often conveys a sense of great physical effort and is usually used when the outcome is likely to be unsuccessful.

LAST/FINAL STRAW
the final thing; the thing or action that is too much or goes too far

1. Constance finally quit her job because the boss asked her to make the coffee and act as a hostess, even though she was hired as an accountant. The *last straw* came when the boss asked her to go out and buy his family's Christmas presents and then complained because she couldn't get her work done.

2. First the builder dropped paint on their new carpet, then he backed his ladder through their window. When he backed his truck over their prized flowerbed, it was the *final straw*, and they told him not to come back.

Synonym: *straw that broke the camel's back*

Both expressions suggest the idea of loading straw (a relatively light material) onto a camel's back until one final light straw (the last straw) breaks the camel's back.

LAUGH ALL THE WAY TO THE BANK
to be proved right or successful in the face of scorn, particularly as regards money

1. No one wanted to invest in Paul's scheme to make money, because they thought it sounded crazy. When it worked, he *laughed all the way to the bank*.

2. People think Mrs. Walker is silly to save money now for her retirement, but she'll *laugh all the way to the bank* when she has a comfortable lifestyle later.

Compare to: *have the last laugh*

The expression suggests that the person who triumphs enjoys laughing at those who doubted him while he takes the fruits of his success (money) to the bank. He will be the rich one.

LAY AN EGG
to do something embarrassing

1. I really *laid an egg* when I asked that elderly woman how old she was. I was just curious, but I should have known it was the wrong thing to do.
2. Everyone stopped talking and looked at the young man in disbelief when he asked Mr. Thomas about his salary. The young man had really *laid an egg*.

Compare to: *bomb*

Whereas *bomb* is usually applied to creative activities (e.g., a play, a book, a movie, an idea) that fail on a grand scale, *lay an egg* is usually applied to something that is socially embarrassing on a small scale.

LAY DOWN THE LAW
to set rules and regulations

1. The boss had noticed that the employees frequently took more time than they were allowed for lunch and coffee breaks. The boss knew he had to put a stop to it, so he called a meeting and *laid down the law*.
2. The teacher decided that he would no longer tolerate late homework, coming late to class, or chatting during class. When the students were all in their seats, he *laid down the law*.

Synonyms: *put (one's) foot down*

Read (someone) the riot act implies more noisy anger against a past action than *lay down the law*, which implies stern instruction governing future behavior.

LAY (ONE'S) CARDS ON THE TABLE
to be open and honest; to reveal everything

1. They didn't understand what Mr. Palmer's plan would lead to or why he was trying to involve them, so finally they asked him to *lay his cards on the table*.
2. When the boss had been strangely quiet for several weeks, the workers knew that something must have been going on. One day she called a meeting and told them that now she could *lay her cards on the table*.

The expression originates from the idea of a card game in which one must reveal one's cards by laying them on the table.

LEAD (SOMEONE) AROUND BY THE NOSE
to dominate someone; to force someone to do something

1. The department chairman runs the department, and no one else has any say in how things are done. He *leads everyone by the nose*.
2. The students seem to be in control of what's going on in the classroom. They *lead the teacher around by the nose*.

LEARN THE ROPES
to become familiar with a task or situation

1. The bank manager told the new trainee to keep his eyes open and watch what the other tellers did until he *learned the ropes*.
2. I'm willing to work long hours and I'll work for free. I'm anxious to *learn the ropes* of this business.

Synonym: *learn the ins and outs*

Compare to: *know the ropes*

These expressions are similar, but take place at different times. Before one *knows the ropes*, one *learns the ropes*.

LEAVE NO STONE UNTURNED
to search everywhere

1. The boss called the employees together for a meeting. He said he didn't know who was stealing from the company, but that he would *leave no stone unturned* until he found out who it was.
2. The police looked everywhere for the prisoner who had escaped. They *left no stone unturned*, but they were unable to find him.

Synonym: *beat the bushes*

The expression suggests that whatever one is searching for might be under a stone, and that one will search so thoroughly as to turn over every stone looking for it.

LEAVE (SOMEONE) [GET LEFT IN] THE LURCH
to abandon someone to a difficult situation, forcing him or her to take all the responsibility

1. The builder hired several carpenters and electricians to work on the building, but he *left them in the lurch* when it came time to pay them.
2. The company went bankrupt and the stockholders got *left in the lurch*. They had to pay all the outstanding bills.
3. Where were you at four o'clock? I thought you were going to attend the meeting and help us with the difficult decisions that needed to be made. You shouldn't have *left us in the lurch* like that.

Synonym: *leave (someone) high and dry*

LEAVE (SOMEONE)/GET LEFT OUT IN THE COLD
to shun someone; to exclude someone from a place or activity

1. Mary seemed not to care for anyone else's feelings, and managed to offend just about everyone. Eventually she got *left out in the cold* and no one included her in their plans or parties.
2. I don't know what I did wrong, but I'd like to make up for it. Please don't *leave me out in* the *cold*.

The expression suggests that when a person is excluded from the group or mainstream, he or she is outside, where it is cold.

LEAVE (SOMEONE) HIGH AND DRY
abandoned or stranded; helpless

1. Bob got a ride to the party with his friends, but they left without him and he had no way to get home. They *left him high and dry.*

2. When you buy a package vacation trip through a travel agency, be sure that it is a company that has a good reputation. Too many companies have gone out of business, leaving those who have already paid their money *high and dry.*

Synonyms: *leave (someone) in the lurch*

Similar to: *leave (someone) holding the bag*

The expression probably originates from the idea of a ship stranded on high ground, leaving it out of water (dry).

LEAVE (SOMEONE) HOLDING THE BAG
to leave somebody with unwanted responsibility

1. If I invest my money with you and things go badly, I want to make sure you're going to take responsibility. I don't want you to *leave me holding the bag.*

2. Laura took a risk and it failed, and she was *left holding the bag.*

Similar to: *leave (someone) in the lurch, leave (someone) high and dry.*

LEAVE WELL ENOUGH ALONE
to accept a situation as it is; to avoid trying to improve a situation one's actions might make it worse

1. Her work isn t perfect, but your criticism might just make the situation worse. I recommend that you *leave well enough alone.*

2. I'm a perfectionist, so I can never *leave well enough alone.* Sometimes that is okay, but sometimes it causes me nothing but trouble.

Synonym: *let sleeping dogs lie*

LEND/GIVE (SOMEONE) AN/(ONE'S) EAR
to listen to someone

1. The boss walked into the coffee room where we were chatting and asked us to *lend him an ear.* He wanted us to listen to what he had to say.

2. All the children pulled on the teacher's skirt, begging to hear the news. She finally told them that if they *gave her an ear,* she would tell them what they wanted to hear.

Dating from at least the 1600s, this phrase has consistently meant to listen to or ask someone to listen. It became especially popular after William Shakespeare's play *Julius Caesar,* in which Mark Antony says to a noisy crowd, 'Friends, Romans, Countrymen, lend me your ears' in order to get them to quiet down and listen.

LET SLEEPING DOGS LIE
to not look for trouble or stir up a troublesome situation

1. The situation seems to have resolved itself, and I'm not going to bring it up again. I'm going to *let sleeping dogs lie.*

2. The politician resigned his office before his colleagues could bring charges of misconduct against him. After that, they *let sleeping dogs lie* and didn't pursue the matter.

Synonym: *leave well enough alone*

The expression is from a proverb dating back to the 13th century and suggests the threat of attack to one who frightens a dog by suddenly waking it from its sleep.

LET THE CAT OUT OF THE BAG
to reveal a secret

1. When Rachel decided she was going to quit her job, she told her best friend but she didn't want to *let the cat out of the bag.* Rachel told her friend not to tell anyone.

2. The children put their money together to buy their mother a birthday present, but the youngest child became excited and couldn't keep from telling his mother what they had bought. His brothers and sisters told him he shouldn't have *let the cat out of the bag.*

Synonym: *spill the beans*

Antonym: *keep (something) under (one's) hat*

Centuries ago, merchants would sell piglets in bags. If a dishonest merchant placed a cat in the bag instead of the more costly and valuable piglet, the buyer might not know until they opened the bag and *let the cat out.*

LETTER PERFECT
exactly right

1. The boss was always happy with Meg's typing because it was *letter perfect.*

2. The actor practiced his lines over and over so that he wouldn't make any mistakes on stage. He wanted to get his lines *letter perfect.*

The expression is used only in reference to writing or speech.

LIFE OF RILEY
the good life; a comfortable life

1. When Henry retires, he plans to live the *life of Riley.* He won't have to work and he'll be able to putter around the garden every day.

2. Mrs. Hartley lived the *life of Riley* until her husband died and she had to take on two jobs to support herself.

Similar to: *lap of luxury*

The lap of luxury means a very comfortable life because one is rich, whereas *the life of Riley is* an easy-going life because one doesn't have to work or isn't working. Someone who is poor can lead *the life of Riley* if he or she doesn't mind being poor. The expression *the life of Riley* seems to originate from a song that was popular in the 1880s. It was a comic song called "Is That Mr. Reilly?" written by Pat Rooney, and it described what Mr. Reilly would do if he suddenly became rich.

LIKE WATER OFF A DUCK'S BACK
having no effect on someone

1. Patricia never takes criticism personally. She accepts it and doesn't feel hurt—it's like *water off a duck's back.*

2. When I told my husband that the storm had ripped off a large part of our roof, the news was like *water off a duck's back*. He said, "It could have been worse."

Similar to: *roll with the punches; take (something) in stride*

The expression suggests that something has no effect in the same way that water rolls off a duck's back, not penetrating the bird's feathers.

LION'S SHARE, THE
the greater part; most

1. The children ate *the lion's share* of the ice cream. They left only a few spoonfuls for their parents.

2. The son inherited *the lion's share* of his father's estate when the old man died. The other relatives in the family got practically nothing.

The expression suggests that the amount of food that a lion would take for itself would be the greatest portion.

LIVE AND LET LIVE
to live without interference from other; to not interfere with the lives of others

1. They were very good neighbors because they never complained or worried about how other people looked after their houses. Their attitude was *live and let live.*

2. Don't tell me how to run my life and I won't tell you how to run yours. Let's *live and let live.*

LOCK, STOCK, AND BARREL
everything; the entirety

1. When the farmer moved away, he sold his land, his farmhouse, his livestock and all his equipment. He sold everything *lock, stock, and barrel.*

2. The shop owner arrived at his shop one morning to find that thieves had stolen all his merchandise. They had cleaned him out *lock, stock, and barrel.*

Synonym: *whole kit and caboodle*

Compare to: *go whole hog; hook, line, and sinker; whole nine yards*

LONG AND SHORT OF IT, THE
the outcome; the point

1. I don't have a lot of time, so please don t go into all the details of the story. What's *the long and short of it?*

2. The assistant manager told the boss that he felt unappreciated and underpaid, that nobody respected him, and that nobody listened to his ideas. Finally he said, *"The long and short of it* is that I'm going to find another job."

Compare to: *bottom line; nitty gritty; make a long story short*

LONG SHOT
an attempt at something that has only a small chance of being successful

1. The newspaper reporter didn't know where the actor was staying. It was a *long shot,* but he guessed that it would be a hotel near the movie studio. He found the actor at the second hotel he called.

2. When they found a house that they really wanted to buy, they called the owners, but found out that they were not interested in selling. It had been a *long shot, so* they weren't too disappointed.

LOOK A GIFT HORSE IN THE MOUTH, NOT
to find fault with a gift or to refuse a gift, usually because one is suspicious of the giver's motives

1. You are too suspicious of Greg's motives. If I were you, I would accept his gift graciously. *Don't look a gift horse in the mouth.*

2. Johanna said that she appreciated their thoughtfulness in giving her a new car, and that she didn't want to *look a gift horse in the mouth,* but she really would prefer a model with a few more extra features like air-conditioning and a CD player.

Don't look a gift horse in the mouth is often used to tell someone that he is being overly suspicious of the giver's motives or overly critical of the gift. The expression originates from the practice of checking the age of a horse by inspecting its teeth. If a person received a horse as a gift and then checked its teeth to see how old it was, this would be seen by the giver as greedy and ungrateful.

LOOK DOWN (ONE'S) NOSE AT (SOMEONE/SOMETHING)
to be snobbish about someone or something

1. The well-off people in this city *look down their noses* at taking public transportation. They only take taxis.

2. The girl's parents would not let her marry the young man because he was from a lower social class. They *looked down their noses* at him.

The expression suggests that one person is on a higher (social) level and must look down his nose in order to see the person or thing on the lower level.

LOOK/FEEL LIKE DEATH WARMED OVER
to look/feel ill or exhausted

1. Sue *looked like death warmed over* when we went to see her in the hospital after her surgery.
2. I stayed up for three nights straight studying for my philosophy exam and now I *feel like death warmed over.*

The expression suggests how a person would look or feel if he or she were warmed up after dying, i.e., still dead.

LOOK LIKE THE CAT THAT SWALLOWED THE CANARY
to have a knowing and self-satisfied smile on one's face; to be pleased with oneself, often because one has done something which one knows was wrong but which was very enjoyable

1. The clever businessman had just completed a very profitable deal for a very good price, and he was very pleased with himself. He *looked like the cat that swallowed the canary.*
2. When the teacher came into the classroom, the students sat there *looking like cats that swallowed the canaries.* The teacher knew the students must be planning something mischievous.

Canaries are songbirds that people keep as pets in cages. A cat that had swallowed a canary would be pleased with itself but also know that it would be in trouble when the master of the house came home and discovered what had happened.

LOOK SHARP
to have a neat and orderly appearance (sentence 1) or to have a stylish appearance (sentence 2)

1. The army drill sergeant shouted at his troops to stand straight, pull in their stomachs, put their heads up and pull their shoulders back. Then he yelled, *"Look sharp."*
2. The boss used to be a pretty sloppy dresser, but now he wore stylish slacks, silk ties, nice shoes, and top-quality jackets. He really *looked sharp.*

LOSE (ONE'S) COOL
to become angry

1. When another soccer player tripped Mary and the referee didn't notice, Mary *lost her cool* and shoved the other girl back.
2. I know you think Tom stole your idea, but you can't lose your temper in this meeting. Don't *lose your cool.*

Synonym: *lose (one's) temper*

Antonym: *keep one's cool*

LOSE/HOLD (ONE'S) TEMPER
to become suddenly angry. To hold one's temper means to remain calm when irritated.

1. The children's mother was tired of asking them to pick up their toys. Finally, she *lost her temper* and yelled at them.
2. Joel was a calm and quiet person who never became visibly angry. Even when pushed, he was always able to *hold his temper.*

Synonym: *lose/keep (one's) cool*

Compare to: *blow (one's) stack; fly off the handle; see red; hot under the collar*

LOW MAN ON THE TOTEM POLE
the person of lowest rank

1. Sheila eventually wanted to become a manager, but since she had just joined the company, she would have to be *low man on the totem pole* for now.
2. Chris was happy when he finally got a promotion in the company. He was no longer *low man on the totem pole.*

The expression originates from the totem poles of some tribes of Native Americans. They were wooden statues made of tree trunks, which consisted of several carved heads, one on top of the other. The expression is usually used to describe the hierarchy in a business, club or office rather than a social or family setting. Even when the expression refers to a female, the expression is still *low man on the totem pole.*

LUCKY DOG/STIFF
a lucky person

1. They got to the airport late and, because there were no more economy seats left, they got to sit in first class for no extra charge. They sure were *lucky dogs.*
2. Carl has relatives who own a car dealership, so he always gets a good deal when he buys a new car. He's a *lucky stiff.*

This slang expression is used between friendly equals.

M

MAKE A CLEAN BREAST OF IT
to admit and explain some wrongdoing; to confess something

1. The thief admitted to the judge that he was guilty and told him the whole story of his crime. He *made a clean breast of it.*

2. The children had lied about taking the candy without permission. They eventually went to their father and *made a clean breast of it,* telling him everything.

Compare to: *wipe the slate clean; get something off (one's) chest*

Whereas *make a clean breast of it* concerns a wrongdoing, *get something off one's chest* refers more generally to one's troubles, worries, or concerns. The expression suggests that guilt is kept in one's breast (heart) and that by revealing one's guilt, one cleans one's breast.

MAKE A LONG STORY SHORT
to summarize; to tell only the main points

1. To *make a long story short,* I think your idea is terrible.

2. He tried to *make a long story short,* but she wouldn't let him finish.

MAKE A MOUNTAIN OUT OF A MOLEHILL
to exaggerate the importance of something; to react more strongly to a situation than is reasonably called for

1. I know you feel hurt because Jean didn't invite you to her wedding, but it was a very small wedding, with just family members and very close friends. You're *making a mountain out of a molehill* if you get upset about it.

2. The clerk gave me the wrong item, then he charged me the wrong price and gave me the wrong change. Should I complain to the manager about him, or am I *making a mountain out of a molehill?*

A molehill is a very small pile of dirt made by a small animal, a mole, which digs tunnels underground. To think that a molehill is as large as a mountain is to greatly exaggerate.

MAKE ENDS MEET
to manage financially; to have enough money for one's basic needs

1. We can hardly pay the rent, buy enough food, and keep the children in clothing. We're barely *making ends meet.*

2. Roger was unable to support his family on his teacher's salary. He *made ends meet* by taking a second job.

Synonym: *get by*

Compare to: *keep (one's) head above water*

Both *keep one's head above water* and *make ends meet* mean having just enough money but no extra, although the former conveys a feeling of desperation. *Keep one's head above water* can also mean survival in situations other than financial, whereas *make ends meet* is limited to financial survival.

MAKE HEADS OR TAILS OF (SOMETHING)
to understand something

1. I can't hear you clearly because the telephone connection is bad. I can t *make heads or tails of* what you're saying.

2. First Louise turned the book one way, then the other. She couldn't *make heads or tails of* the picture she was looking at.

The head is the top or front of something, while the tail is the bottom or back. In use since the 1600s, the phrase *make heads or tails of something* means to understand it from beginning to end (top to bottom). The expression is usually used in the negative or in question form.

MAKE (ONE'S) BLOOD BOIL
to cause someone to become extremely angry

1. I had told Fred never to borrow my car without permission again, but he did it anyway. That *makes my blood boil.*

2. The secretary could hardly believe what one of the office workers had said about her. She was angrier than she could ever remember being before. It *made her blood boil.*

Compare to: *hopping mad; hot under the collar; boiling point*

The expression suggests that when one is very angry, one's blood gets so hot that it boils.

MAKE (ONE'S) MOUTH WATER
to make one salivate in anticipation of something good

1. The chocolate in the display window looks delicious. It *makes my mouth water.*

2. Charles had been saving his money, and now he was so close to being able to buy the sports car he wanted, it *made his mouth water.* He could practically taste it.

The expression is often used in reference to something good to eat (sentence 1), but it can also be used figuratively (sentence 2).

MAKE OR BREAK
to be the deciding factor in whether something succeeds or fails

1. The Smiths were about to sell their house, but the buyers didn't like the color. The Smiths decided to give it a new coat of paint at no extra cost, in case painting the house might *make or break* the deal.

2. Susan decided to study for the test through the night. She knew that her grade on this test would *make or break* her chances of getting admitted to graduate school.

Compare to: *turning point*

MAKE (SOMETHING) FROM SCRATCH
to make something by putting together the separate basic components, rather than using a mix or kit or buying something pre-made

1. My mother never buys cake mixes or ready-made cookies at the supermarket. She always buys the flour, sugar, butter, and eggs, and *makes cakes and cookies from scratch.*

2. George didn't use a kit from a store to build a playhouse for his children. Instead, he designed the playhouse himself, bought all the materials he needed, and *made it from scratch.*

Compare to: *start from scratch*

The expression *make something from scratch* is usually used to describe baked goods (sentence 1). Something *made from scratch* is considered to be superior to something pre-made, because it is probably made more carefully and with the best ingredients.

MAKE THE GRADE
to meet standards; to be satisfactory

1. Of the ten semifinalists in the competition, only three *made the grade* to become finalists.

2. At the end of many manufacturing processes, people check the quality of the goods produced. If the final products don't *make the grade*, they have to be thrown out.

Synonym: *up to snuff*

Compare to: *cut the mustard*

Whereas *make the grade* and *up to snuff* can be used to describe both people (sentence 1) and things (sentence 2), *cut the mustard* is usually used with people.

MAKE TRACKS
to leave, usually quickly

1. We have no reason to stay around, so let's get going. Let's *make tracks.*

2. The boys were playing catch when they accidentally broke one of Mr. Carson's front windows. You've never seen two boys *make tracks* as fast as they did.

Compare to: *beat a hasty retreat*

MARK TIME
to wait out one's time by doing the minimum and without progressing

1. Richard isn't interested in making a career out of the army. He's just putting in the minimum amount of time, *marking time* until he can leave.

2. Carol doesn't particularly care for the job she has now, so she's decided to *mark time* until the job she really wants comes along.

The expression originates from the military command "Mark time!" in which soldiers march in place, i.e., move their feet up and down (go through the motions of marching) without moving forward.

METHOD TO (ONE'S) MADNESS
explanation; forethought or logic

1. There is some *method to her madness*. It's just difficult to understand her way of doing things.

2. There is a *method to my madness*. I like to work on difficult jobs in the morning, when I have the most energy. I save all the simple, boring tasks in the evening, when I need less brain power.

Antonym: *rhyme or reason, no*

MIDAS TOUCH
the ability to make money or to be successful at everything one becomes involved in

1. Everything Linda does is a success. She really has *the Midas touch.*

2. When it comes to investing money and buying stocks, they have *the Midas touch*. It seems like everything they buy goes up in value.

The expression originates from the story of Midas, a mythological king of Phrygia, who was given the power to turn anything he touched into gold.

MILLSTONE AROUND (ONE'S) NECK
a burden or handicap, or a source of worry or concern

1. My elderly parents' house is a *millstone around my neck*. They are unable to keep it up and I have to do all the repairs myself or pay someone to do them for me. I wish they would sell the house and rent an apartment instead.

2. This year's taxes have become a *millstone around my neck*. If I had just gotten them done early, they wouldn't be stressing me out now.

Synonym: *albatross around (one's) neck*

A millstone is a very heavy stone on which one grinds grain in a mill. If a millstone were tied around one's neck, it would be a great burden.

MIND (ONE'S) OWN BUSINESS
to not inquire about, become involved in, or interfere with other people's affairs

1. Sarah started to ask them some very personal questions. They told her to *mind her own business.*

2. They were just sitting on the bus bench, *minding their own business*, when a stranger approached them and started telling them his life story.

Synonyms: *none of (one's) business!*

Antonym: *stick (one's) nose in*

The expression *mind your own business* is a common response of annoyance at a prying or rude inquiry. It is a very direct, even rude, response, and is only used between people of equal social standing.

MISS THE BOAT

to miss an opportunity because one is too late

1. I saw the furniture advertised on sale, but I didn't get to the store in time to buy it. I *missed the boat* on that one.
2. Daniel plans to apply for college at the last possible moment. If he doesn't allow himself enough time, he's going to *miss the boat*.

MONEY TO BURN

extra money; money to spend however one likes

1. The company managers are taking us all out to an expensive restaurant for lunch. They must have *money to burn!*
2. I have to be careful how I spend my money. I don't have *money to burn*.

The expression suggests that one has so much extra money that one can afford to burn it.

MONKEY AROUND

to play like a monkey, i.e., climb on or examine things with curiosity

1. The children have to play in their bedroom. The living room is not for them to *monkey around* in.
2. Steve likes to *monkey around* with old cars to see if he can fix them.

Compare to: *monkey business; clown around; horse around; fool around*

Monkey around emphasizes curiosity or the climbing aspect of play whereas *horse around* emphasizes the physical nature of play and *clown around* means to act silly. *Fool around* is the most general of these and could substitute for the other three.

MONKEY BUSINESS

suspicious activity (sentence 1) or mischievous activity (sentence 2)

1. The boss wasn't sure, but he suspected that there was some *monkey business* going on with the company accounts.
2. The children had become very quiet in the playroom and their mother decided it was time to see what kind of *monkey business* they were up to.

Synonym: *hanky-panky*

Compare to: *monkey around*

MORE THAN MEETS THE EYE

some hidden aspect to a situation

1. I can't see any reason why this man on the telephone is trying to give me a free vacation. *There's more here than meets the eye.*
2. When Jerry had received a letter saying that the company was letting him go, the reason the letter gave was a lack of work, but Jerry had been busier than ever these last few months. He thought to himself, "There's *more to this than meets the eye.*"

MORE (SOMETHING) THAN (ONE) BARGAINED FOR

more than one expected

1. I agreed to join a book club because the saleswoman said I didn't have to buy any book I didn't want, but I was shocked when I learned I had to spend a certain amount of money every month. It was *more of a commitment than I bargained for*.
2. I thought you were looking forward to being in the army. Was it *more work than you bargained for?*

The expression is often used in a negative sense, i.e., more money, more trouble, more work, etc. than one expected or wanted.

MORE THAN ONE WAY TO SKIN A CAT, THERE'S

there are different ways to accomplish the same thing; there are different possible solutions to a problem

1. There must be some way to raise enough money to buy a car. We've put all our savings together but it isn't enough. Still, there's *more than one way to skin a cat*. I'll get a second job!
2. My friends asked me how they could accomplish something that seemed impossible. I told them that they simply hadn't looked at all the possibilities. I told them there's always *more than one way to skin a cat* and that they would eventually find a solution.

MOVE HEAVEN AND EARTH

to try very hard to do something

1. The young man was accused of a terrible crime. His parents were convinced that he was innocent and swore they would *move heaven and earth* to get him acquitted.
2. Linda's daughter is getting married on Friday, the same day Linda gets back from an out-of-town business trip. She will *move heaven and earth* to get to the wedding on time.

The expression suggests how hard one would have to try if one tried to move things as big as heaven and earth.

N

NECK OF THE WOODS
an area; a place

1. I don't recognize you and I know just about everyone in this town. You must not be from this *neck of the woods*.

2. Excuse me. Can you give me directions? I'm not familiar with this *neck of the woods*.

The expression is often used to describe what part of the country a person comes from, but it can also be used to describe unfamiliarity with a part of a city or state. It is frequently used in a negative structure.

NEED (SOMETHING) LIKE (ONE) NEEDS A HOLE IN THE HEAD
to have absolutely no need for something

1. Bonita arrived at work to find a new stack of papers on her desk. "*I need more work like I need a hole in the head,*" she complained.

2. Don't subscribe to another magazine, since you already receive more magazines than you can possibly read. You *need a new magazine like you need a hole in the head.*

The expression, which comes from Yiddish, is ironic. One certainly wouldn't want or need a hole in one's head, and one wants or needs the thing in question just as little.

NIP (SOMETHING) IN THE BUD
to stop something before it becomes big or involved; to stop something before it gets much of a start

1. My three-year-old son has become rude and demanding. I don't like his bad behavior and I'm going to *nip it in the bud* before it gets any worse.

2. The boss wasn't happy with a few of his workers who had begun to leave the office before quitting time. He was afraid they would fall into the habit of leaving early if he didn't *nip it in the bud,* so he told them they would have to stop.

The expression compares stopping a bad situation to cutting (nipping) a flower before it has a chance to grow (while it is still a bud).

NITTY-GRITTY, THE
the heart of the issue; the most important part of the discussion; the essential points

1. These conferences always begin with introductory speeches that don't say much. I'm glad when they're finished and the speakers get down to *the nitty-gritty*—that's when we really learn something new.

2. Let's skip the small talk, and go straight to *the nitty-gritty*: what price do you want for the car, and when will you be able to part with it?

Compare to: *get down to brass tacks; bottom line; long and short of it*

NIX (SOMETHING)
to cancel an idea or plan; to reject or forbid something

1. I thought it was an excellent idea, but he *nixed it.* Now we are back to where we started.

2. Every time I ask my parents if I can visit my cousins, they *nix* my request. They think my cousin is a bad influence on me.

Synonym: *give (something) the thumbs down*

NONE OF (ONE'S) BUSINESS
private; not for anybody else to know

1. You keep asking me how much money I have, but I don't want to tell you. It's *none of your business*.

2. I wish my sister would stop asking questions about my personal life. It's *none of her business*.

NOT HAVE A LEG TO STAND ON
to be in an indefensible situation or to have no support for an argument or case

1. Some of the workers accused Louis of stealing from the company, but they *didn't have a leg to stand on*. He had never stolen from the company and they had no proof that he had.

2. Stop trying to persuade me that you didn't start the fight. You *don't have a leg to stand on*. All the children saw the whole thing, and they told me exactly how it happened.

Having a leg to stand on lends support to something, and *not having a leg to stand on* means support is lacking.

NOTHING TO WRITE HOME ABOUT
ordinary; so-so; not especially good or important

1. Tom's parents wanted to know how he liked the school. Tom said the school was all right, but it was *nothing to write home about.*

2. When we asked them about their trip, they said they couldn t complain about it but the hotel was *nothing to write home about.*

Antonyms: *something to crow about; a feather in one's cap.*

The expression originates from the idea that if one were writing a letter to one's family, the person or thing or event in question is so ordinary or insignificant that one wouldn't even mention it in the letter.

NOT (ONE'S) CUP OF TEA
not to suit someone; not to one's liking

1. I like going to parks and doing things outdoors. Going to museums and galleries just *isn't my cup of tea.*

2. The man JoAnn met at the party was nice, but he wasn't *her cup of tea.*

The expression is usually used in the negative.

NOT WORTH A DIME
worthless

1. Scott thought that he could sell his collection of comic books to make some extra money, but then he learned that everybody else already had the same comic books. His collection *wasn't worth a dime.*

2. Police caught the diamond thief when he tried to sell a fake diamond. It was *not worth a dime.*

Synonyms: *not worth a dime, not worth a hill of beans, not worth the paper it's printed on, not worth a plugged nickel*

This expression is always used in the negative.

NOT WORTH A HILL OF BEANS
worthless

1. If you don't follow through on what you say, your word is *not worth a hill of beans.*

2. You should take good care of that car. If it stops running properly, it's *not worth a hill of beans.*

Synonyms: *not worth a dime; not worth a red cent; not worth a plugged nickel; not worth the paper it's printed on*

This expression is always used in the negative.

NOT WORTH A PLUGGED NICKEL
worthless

1. The millionaire invested in oil wells that proved to be dry. They *weren't worth a plugged nickel.*

2. I bought this house before I knew it was located on a toxic waste site. Now it *isn't worth a plugged nickel.*

Synonyms: *not worth a dime; not worth a red cent; not worth a hill of beans; not worth the paper it's printed on*

This expression is always used in the negative.

NOT WORTH A RED CENT
worthless

1. That coupon is expired, so the grocery store won't accept it. It's *not worth a red cent.*

2. A telephone directory from thirty years ago isn't going to help you find what you need. It's *not worth a red cent.*

Synonyms: *not worth a dime; not worth a plugged nickel; not worth a hill of beans; not worth the paper it's printed on*

This expression is always used in the negative.

NOT WORTH THE PAPER IT'S PRINTED ON
worthless

1. If you miss the train, you can't just go at another time. Your ticket *won't be worth the paper it's printed on.*

2. Make sure you spend or exchange all of your money before we leave this country; once we leave, it *isn't worth the paper it's printed on.*

Synonyms: *not worth a dime; not worth a plugged nickel; not worth a hill of beans; not worth a red cent*

This expression is always used in the negative and usually refers to documents or money, i.e., things printed on paper.

O

ODD MAN OUT

the person who is left out; the person who doesn't fit in

1. An uneven number of boys wanted to play the game, so that when both teams had chosen the same number of players, one boy was left standing in the middle. John was the *odd man out*.

2. I felt as though I didn t belong with the group of people at the party. I was *odd man out*.

The expression probably originates from the idea of choosing up two sides for a game in which both teams need an even number of players. If there were an uneven number of people wanting to play, the last (odd) person was left out. The expression has broadened in its meaning to describe anyone who is not included or made to feel part of a group. When the expression is used to describe a woman, the word "man" does not become "woman".

ODDS AND ENDS

small items that are left over, don't match, or are missing a mate

1. The repair shop is full of *odds and ends* that Mr. Bell collects and keeps just in case he can use them to fix something else.

2. I keep all my *odds and ends* in this drawer, but it's becoming so full of junk that I can't find anything anymore.

OFF (ONE'S) ROCKER

out of one's mind; slightly crazy

1. Mrs. Crowell is convinced she sees ghosts in the halls, and that they talk to her. I think she's *off her rocker*.

2. You must be *off your rocker* to think that the boss will give you such a big pay raise. He hasn't given anyone else a raise like that.

Compare to: *bats in (one's) belfry; out to lunch; screw loose*

All of these expressions, including *off one's rocker,* are used in a light-hearted, slightly humorous sense.

OFF THE BEATEN PATH/TRACK

off the road or way that is most often chosen by other people

1. Jennifer likes to take her vacations in the major resorts where everyone goes. She likes the big and noisy crowds instead of places that are *off the beaten track.*

2. Alex has never followed the crowd or done things just to please others. His way in life has been *off the beaten path.*

The expression can be used either literally (as in sentence 1) or figuratively (as in sentence 2).

OFF THE CUFF

without much advance preparation; spontaneously

1. Holly is a great speaker. Most people like to plan their speeches carefully in advance, but Holly prefers to speak *off the cuff.* Even so, her speeches are always a great success.

2. I can't give you an exact figure for the number of students we have at the university, but *off the cuff* I'd say about 25,000.

Synonym: *off the top of (one's) head*

Compare to: *on the spur of the moment*

Off the cuff is usually applied to speaking or writing. *On the spur of the moment* means that one makes a decision to do something suddenly and therefore without much preparation.

OFF THE TOP OF (ONE'S) HEAD

to say something without much advance preparation

1. Melissa didn t know how many people had called, but guessing *off the top of her head,* she said about a hundred.

2. Richard was unsure what kind of advertising campaign the company wanted, but he made a suggestion *off the top of his head* and they liked it.

Synonym: *off the cuff*

OFF THE WALL

unusual; peculiar

1. Most of Kevin's suggestions are sound and practical but a few of them are really *off the wall*. I wonder how he comes up with them.

2. Some dress designers today are designing fashionable clothes that are *off the wall*. I prefer classic designs, and I can't imagine wearing some of those bizarre fashions.

Antonym: *run of the mill*

OLD-BOY NETWORK

the male connections that a man acquires, usually while in college or the military, later used to disseminate jobs and information

1. Mr. Turner got his job through the *old-boy network,* which consisted of the friends he knew when he was at the university.

2. Sometimes it can be very hard to get hired by certain companies because they depend so heavily on hiring through an *old-boy network*. If you aren't a part of it, you don't have a chance.

An *old-boy network* serves as a way to get jobs and spread information, sometimes to the exclusion of others who are outside the network.

OLD FUDDY-DUDDY

a person who is old-fashioned and not open to new technology or ideas

1. Tom is a bit of an *old fuddy-duddy*. He refuses to get a mobile phone or a computer.

2. My music teacher is pretty cool, but my history teacher is an *old fuddy-duddy*.

Similar to: *stuffed shirt*

Describing someone as an *old fuddy-duddy* is usually seen as harmless and humorous, whereas calling someone a *stuffed shirt* can be rude. The expression can refer to either a woman or a man.

OLD HAT

routine to the point of boredom (sentence 1); old-fashioned and outmoded (sentence 2)

1. Every New Year's Eve, we go to the same restaurant for dinner and the same hotel for dancing. It's getting to be *old hat* and I'm tired of it. Let's do something different this year.

2. I've heard that idea a thousand times before. It's *old hat*. Can't you think of anything new and different that we could try?

Synonyms: *in a rut; on a treadmill*

ON A/THE WARPATH/RAMPAGE

looking for a fight; very angry and upset with someone or something

1. I decided to get out of the house until my father calms down. He was really *on the warpath* when he saw that I had damaged his new car.

2. The manager is *on a rampage* because he found out that the company management doesn't plan on keeping him when they close his department. He's really angry.

The expression originally referred to American Indians, who were described as *on the warpath* (literally on the way to war) when they were preparing for a fight.

ON CLOUD NINE

blissfully happy

1. Sharon loved horses, and when she finally took her first riding lesson, she was *on cloud nine*.

2. Seth might be angry if you interrupt his video game—it's new, and he's *on cloud nine*.

Synonym: *seventh heaven, in*

ON HOLD, PUT (SOMETHING)

to postpone something; to wait until later (sentences 1 and 2); to ask somebody to wait without hanging up the telephone (sentence 3)

1. We had planned to start building the new shopping center next month, but the company's profits are down so the project has been *put on hold* for a while.

2. Lorraine was having second thoughts about marrying Phil before both of them finished college. She told him she thought they should put the wedding *on hold* for a few years.

3. I've been trying to call the doctor, but his secretary keeps putting me *on hold*. I don't have time to wait for the doctor to come to the phone, so I guess I'll try to call him again later.

Synonyms: *on the back burner; on ice*

On hold specifically refers to postponing some action, whereas *put something on ice* means to store or reserve some item for later use. Something that is *on the back burner* has a lower priority or is less important than something else.

ON ICE, PUT (SOMETHING)

to put something (an excess of some item) in reserve for later use

1. We didn t need all the money we had raised, so we decided to *put some of it on ice* until our funds were low.

2. I'm glad we found enough supplies to do the job, but I wish we had enough to *put some on ice*. We will need some next year too, and we may not be able to find any then.

Synonyms: *salt (something) away; save (something) for a rainy day; on the back burner; on hold*

ON/OFF A/THE TREADMILL

in a dull and boring routine

1. Mr. Jones goes to work and does the same old job every day, and he never does anything different. He's *on a treadmill*.

2. Everyone thinks I'm so predictable, but some day I'm going to get *off the treadmill* and do something adventurous.

3. They've been *on the treadmill* their whole lives. They would feel very uncomfortable doing anything spontaneous, so it would be impossible for them to get off and do something different.

Synonym: *in a rut*

Compare to: *old hat*

A treadmill is a machine consisting of a continuous belt or moving steps that circle around and around and to which there is no end. The expression is often used to describe one's job or daily life.

ON (ONE'S) LAST LEGS

about to die, fail, or collapse

1. This car is practically worthless. It's in the repair shop more than it's on the road. I think it's *on its last legs*.

2. The company is selling its assets and is about to declare bankruptcy. It's *on its last legs*.

The expression suggests a person who is about to collapse for the last time because his or her legs no longer have the strength to carry him forward or hold him upright.

ON THE BACK BURNER, PUT (SOMETHING)

to decrease the amount of energy spent on some activity; to delay or postpone action on some activity

1. The boss isn't sure he wants to pursue that new project right now. I think it's *on the back burner* until the current project is finished.
2. Because of the country's debt problems, the government has had to put its plans to expand the national medical program *on the back burner*.

Compare to: *on hold; on ice*

The expression *on the back burner* comes from cooking on a standard stove, which has four burners, two in front and two in back. The burners in front are used for immediate cooking, while the ones in back are often used for simmering or keeping things warm. To move something to the front burner means to make some project highest priority.

ON THE BALL

mentally sharp or alert; well-prepared; efficient

1. You've been making too many mistakes these days. You'd better get *on the ball* if you want to keep your job.
2. I can't seem to concentrate today. I'm just not *on the ball*.

Antonym: *out to lunch*

ON THE BLINK

not working correctly

1. We can't watch the football game at my house. My television is *on the blink*.
2. The clock in the office has been *on the blink* for months. I don't think they'll ever get it fixed.

Synonym: *on the fritz*

The expression is usually used with electronic devices. It is not used with more mechanical devices such as cars or other vehicles.

ON THE FRITZ

not working correctly

1. This television works for a few minutes and then the picture fades out. It's *on the fritz*.
2. We'd better think about getting a new refrigerator, because this one has a puddle of water under it every few days. It seems to be *on the fritz*.

Synonym: *on the blink*

ON THE GO

constantly busy; very active

1. My neighbor has four young children, and she is always driving them somewhere: to school, to dance lessons, to visit friends, to the doctor's. She's always *on the go*.
2. Some food companies now make ready-to-eat breakfast food for people *on the go*. They can just put the food in the microwave oven or toaster and take it with them in the car.

ON THE LEVEL

honest and without deception

1. I know you don't believe me, but what I'm telling you is *on the level*.
2. The car dealer offered Robert a chance to buy a fancy car at a big discount. Robert was suspicious because he didn t know if the deal was really *on the level*.

Compare to: *on the up and up*

ON THE NOSE

exactly

1. Their parents tried not to tell them where they were going, but the children were too clever for them. They guessed it *on the nose*.
2. The children's father told them each to think of a number between one and ten. The child who chose the closest number to the one he was thinking of would get the larger piece of candy. His youngest daughter picked the number *on the nose*.

Compare to: *hit the nail on the head*

ON THE ROCKS

unstable; likely to collapse. When referring to alcoholic beverages, it means with ice cubes

1. I read in the tabloids that those celebrities' relationship is *on the rocks*. I wonder if it can be saved?
2. Mr. Smith was afraid that after the stormy meeting, his relationship with his client was *on the rocks*. He decided to call his client later in the day and try to straighten things out.
3. When Judy goes to a bar, she always orders a drink *on the rocks*.

The expression is often used to describe a long-term relationship or a marriage (sentence 1), but it can also describe a non-romantic relationship (sentence 2). The expression originates with the image of a ship that has been cast against the rocks and is about to break up. When the expression means "with ice" (as in sentence 3), the ice cubes in the glass are being compared to rocks.

ON THE SPOT
in an awkward social situation (sentence 1) or immediately and nearby (sentence 2)

1. I'm sorry to ask you these questions without giving you a chance to prepare—I didn t mean to put you *on the spot*.
2. Sherry thought that the doctor would make a future appointment to give her the shot, but he wanted to do it that day. "We can do it here, *on the spot*," he said.

ON THE TIP OF (ONE'S) TONGUE
almost remembered; about to be said

1. Chris knew the woman, but he couldn't remember her name. It was *on the tip of his tongue*, but it just wouldn't come.
2. Martha was trying to recall the name of the restaurant where they had eaten. It was *on the tip of her tongue* when someone interrupted her thoughts.

The expression is used when one is trying very hard to recall something such as a name, date, word, or fact and feels that he or she is just about to remember it. The expression suggests that the information is so close to being recalled that it is at the front of one's mouth.

ON THE UP AND UP
honest; ethical; fair

1. The salesman offered us an unbelievable price on computer equipment. Do you think his offer is *on the up and up*?
2. Governor Russell is a very honest politician. He would never do anything that was not *on the up and up*.

Compare to: *on the level*

ON THE WAGON
to abstain from drinking alcoholic beverages because one cannot control oneself

1. Peter used to drink alcohol to excess, but now he doesn't drink anymore. He's *on the wagon*.
2. I realized I was an alcoholic some years ago. I finally got help and I've been *on the wagon* ever since.

Antonym: *fall off the wagon*

Similar to: *cold turkey*

The expression *on the wagon* usually describes someone who is unable to handle alcohol or who is an alcoholic rather than a person who chooses to abstain for religious or other personal reasons. *On the wagon* refers to alcoholic drinks whereas *cold turkey* refers to abruptly stopping the intake of drugs, cigarettes, and other habits.

ON THIN ICE, SKATE/TREAD
in an unsafe or risky position

1. Steve is going to run into trouble if he continues to arrive late at work. He's *on thin ice* with the boss already because he spends more time talking on the phone than working.
2. Anita is in serious trouble at the university. Her grades are poor and unless she does well on her final exams, she may be *skating on thin ice*.
3. The children's mother couldn't stand many more of their demands. She told them that they were *treading on thin ice* because they were about to make her lose her temper.

The expression suggests how dangerous it is to tread (walk) or skate on ice that, although frozen, is not thick enough to support one's weight.

ONCE IN A BLUE MOON
very rarely

1. Jean's parents encouraged her to accept the job with the prestigious company in New York. They told her that a job offer like that comes along only *once in a blue moon*.
2. Roger and Sandy like to stay at home. They rarely travel and they almost never go out to dinner, though they go to the movies *once in a blue moon*.

ONE FELL SWOOP
one quick, sweeping action

1. The army surrounded the enemy soldiers without their knowledge, and in *one fell swoop* were able to cut them off from their supplies.
2. Dianne swept in with her presentation, and in *one fell swoop* she garnered the support of every member of the board of directors.

OPEN BOOK
a person who doesn't hide anything about himself or herself; a person's life (sentence 1) or mind in which nothing is hidden

1. Cindy hides nothing about how she spends her time. Her life is an *open book*.
2. James and John are as different as night and day. James is an *open book*, but John is very secretive.

The expression suggests that a person who is an open book is easy to "read" or understand.

OPEN-MINDED
willing to consider new ideas

1. As a new employee, it's important to be *open-minded* and enthusiastic. You aren't expected to know everything about your job yet, but you should be open to learning new things.
2. Kim is definitely an *open-minded* person. She is very tolerant of different attitudes, cultures, and religions.

Antonym: *closed-minded*

Similar to: *open mind, keep an*

OPEN MIND, (KEEP) AN
to be willing to listen to and consider all sides of an issue; not to have made up one's mind in advance

1. Julie's father's mind was made up not to let her have her own car. She said that he didn't have *an open mind* about the matter, and that he had not given her a fair chance to persuade him.
2. I have almost decided to vote for the conservative candidate, but I'm still willing to listen to what the other candidates have to say. I'm trying to *keep an open mind* about all the candidates until election day.

Antonym: *closed-minded*

Open-minded and *closed-minded* generally refer to a person's overall outlook or approach, whereas *keep an open mind* is used to describe one's approach to one particular situation or topic.

OUT OF A CLEAR BLUE SKY
without warning

1. Erica didn't expect James to propose marriage so quickly. For her, the proposal came *out of a clear blue sky*.
2. Spencer hadn t sent his resume out, so when somebody called him for a job interview, the offer came *out of a clear blue sky*.

Synonym: *out of the blue*

OUT OF CIRCULATION
removed from the public; no longer available for use or social interaction

1. This book is no longer available in the library. It's *out of circulation*.
2. Mrs. Winter took her husband's sudden death very hard, and she doesn't have the will to get out and get on with life. She's taken herself *out of circulation*.

The expression is usually used to describe a social situation (sentence 2) but probably originated with printed material (sentence 1).

OUT OF ONE'S DEPTH/LEAGUE
beyond one's capability

1. I once took part in a chess tournament and got the chance to play a grand master. I lost in just five moves. I was really *out of my league*.
2. After I started my new job, I quickly realized that I was completely *out of my depth*. Nothing I'd learned in school or in my previous jobs had prepared me for the new challenges I had to face.

Synonyms: *bite off more than (one) can chew; in over one's head*

OUT OF (ONE'S) ELEMENT
in a situation that one is unprepared for or unfamiliar with

1. Bob felt *out of his element* at the crowded party. He does much better with small groups of people.
2. The beginning of a presentation is sometimes difficult. You feel *out of your element* standing in front of an audience. But if you've practiced your talk, it gets easier once you get started.

Synonym: *fish out of water*

Antonym: *in (one's) element*

OUT OF THE BLUE
suddenly and unexpectedly

1. We were walking down the street when from *out of the blue* an old classmate we hadn't seen for years appeared.
2. Pam was driving down the highway when, *out of the blue*, a truck crossed in front of her and she had to slam on her brakes.

Synonym: *out of a clear blue sky*

OUT OF THE FRYING PAN AND INTO THE FIRE
from a bad situation to one that is even worse

1. Edith's parents were happy when she broke off her friendship with Ralph, until she started seeing George, who is an even worse influence on her. She's jumped *out of the frying pan into the fire*.
2. Tim didn't like the extra responsibility of being an assistant manager, but now he's decided to accept the position of full manager. He's leaping *out of the frying pan into the fire*.

OUT OF THE WOODS
out of danger; out of a very difficult situation

1. The doctor told the boy's parents that he was no longer in danger of dying—he had made it through the night and his high fever had returned to normal. He was *out of the woods*.
2. The accountant was trying very hard to find a bank that would loan the company money to stay in business. When he found a bank, the company president was relieved, but the accountant told him the company was *not out of the woods* yet.

3. There was quite a scandal brewing, and it looked like it would cause the downfall of several high-ranking government officials. Fred thought he had avoided being touched by the scandal, but he wouldn't be completely sure for a few weeks. He *wasn't out of the woods* yet.

The expression is often used to describe no longer being in danger of dying (sentence 1). It can also be used to describe situations equally critical, such as the demise of a company (sentence 2) or the death of someone's political life (sentence 3).

OUT TO LUNCH

absent-minded, unaware or confused (sentence 1); ignorant on some topic (sentence 2); harmlessly crazy or out of touch with reality (sentence 3)

1. I can't believe I was so absent-minded that I erased my entire hard drive! I'm really *out to lunch.*

2. You don t know what you're talking about! You're *out to lunch.*

3. That old soldier is a little *out to lunch.* He wanders around here telling everyone old war stories as though the war was just yesterday.

Antonym: *on the ball*

Compare to: *know if (one) is coming or going* (sentence 1); *know beans about (something); all wet, for the birds* (sentence 2); *bats in (one's) belfry; off (one's) rocker; screw loose, have a* (sentence 3)

OVER A BARREL

in a difficult situation or position

1. They agreed on the price of the car with the salesman, but now they can't borrow enough from the bank. They're *over a barrel* because they'll lose their deposit if they can t come up with the rest of the money.

2. If I look for another job, the companies I interview with are going to want to check with my current boss. But I don't want him to know I'm looking for a new job. *I'm over a barrel.*

3. I had to borrow some money from a colleague at work, and now he wants me to help him fix his car on Saturday. I really don't have time to do it, but he's got me *over a barrel* since I owe him a favor.

Similar to: *in a bind; in a fix; between a rock and a hard place; between the devil and the deep blue sea*

OVER THE HILL

too old to be of much value

1. My dog liked to play when he was young, but now he sleeps all day. He's *over the hill.*

2. Don't you dare tell me I'm *over the hill.* I may be old but I still feel as young as I did thirty years ago.

Synonym: *past (one's) prime*

The expression is used for people and animals, but not for nonliving things.

OVER THE TOP

beyond expectations; outside normal or accepted boundaries; exaggerated

1. I know my question annoyed him, but his response was *over the top.* He really needs to apologize for his rudeness.

2. Your behavior is sometimes a bit *over the top.* You'll really have to act more appropriately if you ever want to do well in this business.

PAINT (SOMEONE) A PICTURE
to explain something in very great detail

1. Mary is one of those people to whom you have to explain everything in great detail. You always have to *paint her a picture*.

2. I've explained as much as I should have to. Do I have to *paint you a picture*?

The expression conveys the idea that the explanation is as good and as thorough as if one had painted a picture.

PANDORA'S BOX
a situation that contains many unexpected and unwanted problems and consequences

1. Be careful. If you try to find out more than you should about her past, you might be opening *Pandora's box*.

2. Larry thought the sale of his mother's house was a *Pandora's box*. There were too many people to please and too many people who might be offended.

Synonym: *can of worms, open a*

The expression originates from the Greek mythological character Pandora, who was given a box containing all the evils that could befall mankind. She opened it, unleashing all mankind's ills.

PAR FOR THE COURSE
usual or to be expected; typical

1. Robert is late as usual. It's *par for the course*.

2. I asked for five different kinds of sandwiches at the cafeteria, and they didn't have any of them. But that's *par for the course;* they never have half the items listed on the menu.

Compare to: *rule of thumb*

The expression originates from the game of golf, in which *par* is the expected or usual number of strokes a player should take to get the ball from the tee into the hole on that particular course. The expression is usually used in a negative context, i.e. one couldn't expect anything better.

PASS THE BUCK
to redirect the blame or responsibility for something (usually a decision) to someone else

1. Sharon suggested we go to see a movie, which turned out to be awful. Then she tried to *pass the buck* and pretend that it hadn't been her choice.

2. Carol never tries to *pass the buck*. She is always willing to make hard decisions and stand behind them, even if they aren't always the best ones.

In poker games during the 1800s, a shotgun pellet (called buck) or a pocketknife (often made from buckhorn) was passed to the next person responsible for dealing the cards. By the 20th century, *pass the buck* came to mean shifting responsibility to someone else. In 1949, U.S. President Harry Truman placed a sign on his desk that read 'the buck stops here,' meaning that he took responsibility for government actions and would not try to place the responsibility on anybody else.

PAST (ONE'S) PRIME
too old to be of much value

1. As an athlete, he's *past his prime*. He just can't run as fast as he could five years ago.

2. Nancy isn't *past her prime* yet. She still has a lot of energy.

Synonym: *over the hill*

PATIENCE OF JOB
unlimited patience; the willingness to endure hardship patiently

1. Your twins are so mischievous, but you never lose your temper. You have the *patience of Job*.

2. That teacher must have the *patience of Job*—he answers all of the students' questions and waits for them to be quiet before he continues.

The word *Job* is a name (it rhymes with *robe*). The expression originates from the Biblical story of Job, a man who was able to keep his faith despite the hardships God inflicted on him during a contest with the devil.

PAY (SOMEONE) BACK
to respond to somebody's behavior with similar behavior

1. Desmond was rude to you on the playground, but you can be nice to him anyway. You don't have to *pay him back* by insulting him.

2. Shelly appreciated Tim's kind words, and tried to *pay him back* by encouraging him the next time they met.

The expression is often, but not always, used in reference to negative situations.

PAY THE PIPER
to pay for one's mistakes; to live with the consequences of one's (wrong) actions

1. Catherine thought she could play her way through school, and now she has to stay after class to make up her failed grades. She should have known she would have to *pay the piper.*

2. I cheated people out of their money. I got caught, and now I'm in prison, *paying the piper* for what I did.

A piper is a musician who plays on a pipe.

PAY THROUGH THE NOSE
to pay a great amount; to pay too much

1. Carissa wanted tickets to the concert so badly that she was willing to pay double for them. She *paid through the nose*, but she made it to the concert.

2. Peter's parents said he couldn't go out until he finished his chores, so Peter promised to do his sister's chores for a whole week if she would do his for a day. He had to pay *through the nose,* but it was worth it to him.

Compare to: *cost (someone) a mint; cost (someone) an arm and a leg*

The expression usually refers to paying money (sentence 1), but it can also refer to exacting other kinds of payment such as trading work, making someone feel very guilty, etc.

PENCIL/PAPER PUSHER
an office worker; a bureaucrat who routinely does his or her paperwork job without any desire to advance

1. Charlene wanted to get ahead in her job. Although she was a clerk now, she had no intention of being a *pencil pusher* all her life.

2. Most of the employees here are just *paper pushers.* They sit behind their desks, do their jobs, and they don't expect to be anywhere else in ten years.

The expression is derogatory. It is often used to describe someone who ought to be more ambitious.

PENNY PINCHER
a person that doesn't like to spend money

1. My mother won't spend money on new clothes until her old ones are nearly falling apart. She's a *penny pincher.*

2. When Joe decided to save money for a house, he became a *penny pincher*—he stopped eating at restaurants, went to the library instead of buying books, and walked to work instead of taking the train.

PETER OUT
to disappear gradually

1. We followed the river upstream as it got smaller and smaller until it finally *petered out.*

2. The members of the club got together every week until they began to lose interest. At first, just a few people stopped coming, but eventually they all *petered out.*

The expression does not mean to disappear gradually as in fade, but to disappear slowly in terms of quantity or size.

PICK (SOMEONE'S) BRAIN
to get information from someone, usually by questioning the person carefully and in great detail

1. I was exhausted after spending hours with the investigators while they *picked my brain.* Unfortunately, I wasn't able to give them any useful information.

2. You know a lot about the latest in jet engine design, don't you? We want to *pick your brain* about the new design before we start to build our engine.

The expression suggests that a person's brain contains bits of information that can be "picked" like fruit from a tree or like meat off of a bone.

PIE IN THE SKY
something that is unrealistic or that cannot be achieved

1. Don't believe those *pie-in-the-sky* advertisements you see on television selling large plots of land for pennies. They're too good to be true.

2. The salesman promised Amy that the wrinkle cream would make her skin as soft as a baby's, but she knew not to believe him. It was *pie in the sky.*

PIECE OF CAKE, A
something that is easy to do

1. When the children accidentally threw the ball on top of the roof, the gym teacher asked me to climb up and get it down. I told her it would be easy for me. It was *a piece of cake.*

2. When Roger studied Spanish, it was *a piece of cake,* but he found that learning Japanese was very hard.

PINCH PENNIES
to be very careful with one's money; to be concerned about how one spends every penny

1. Joe shops at discount supermarkets and watches for items on sale. He's a real *penny pincher.*

2. They waste gasoline driving an extra ten miles to a store that has something on sale so they can save a dollar. They squander dollars to *pinch pennies.*

The expression is slightly disparaging. A penny is a coin worth one cent in the U.S. This is the smallest denomination in the American monetary system.

PINK SLIP
notice that one has been fired from one's job

1. Yesterday the company fired a dozen people. They all got *pink slips* in their pay packets.

2. Gordon came home early from work looking worried. He had just gotten a *pink slip*, and now he would have to find another job.

The expression probably originates from the color of the form used to notify people that they had been fired. Such forms often came in multiple carbon copies. Each copy was a different color and was designated for a different recipient, e.g., the pay office got one particular color, while the fired person always got the pink copy.

PLAY HARDBALL
to work or act aggressively, competitively, or ruthlessly, as in business or politics

1. You have to be willing to *play hardball* in the business world today. If you aren't aggressive, you'll be taken over by the competition.

2. Mr. Norton had been mayor of a small town for many years, but when he decided to run for Congress his friends told him he would have to be prepared to *play hardball*. National politics can be much more aggressive than local politics.

The expression originates from the game of baseball, which uses a hard ball, as opposed to the similar game of softball.

PLAY IT BY EAR
to go along with a situation as it develops before deciding what to do; to do something without prior planning

1. Let's get in the car and go for a drive. We don't have to decide before we start where we're going; let's just *play it by ear*.

2. I'm going to watch to see how the situation develops and decide what to do as I go along. I want to *play it by ear* and see what happens.

Compare to: *wing it; by the seat of (one's) pants*

The expression probably originates from the idea of playing a piece of music by ear, i.e., not reading the music as one plays but simply listening to the piece, picking out the notes by ear and then playing it.

PLAY (ONE'S) CARDS RIGHT
to do all the right things and make all the right moves in order to achieve some end

1. I can't promise anything, but if you listen carefully and *play your cards right,* I might be able to include you in this deal.

2. The bank guard caught the thief with the money. The thief told the guard that if he *played his cards right* and let the thief go free, he could get half the money.

The expression often suggests something slightly conspiratorial and dishonest. It probably originates from a card game like bridge, in which the players have any number of ways to play their cards, but playing them in just the right way will result in winning.

PLAY SECOND FIDDLE
to be in a subordinate position; to have a lower rank or standing than someone else

1. Jim wasn't very happy when he was made assistant manager while Frank was promoted to manager. Jim didn't want to *play second fiddle* to Frank.

2. Both Ron and Sam liked Julie, but Julie preferred Sam. Ron *played second fiddle* to Sam.

The expression probably originates from the fact that in an orchestra the first violin, or "fiddle," gets most of the attention and plays the leading part, while the second fiddle is less noticed.

PLAY WITH FIRE
to invite disaster by doing something foolish, dangerous, or risky

1. Don't get involved with people who use drugs. Don't *play with fire*.

2. How can Becky go out with that man? He has such a bad reputation. Doesn't she know she's *playing with fire?*

POKER FACE
an expressionless face; a face that reveals nothing of one's feelings or thoughts

1. Kay isn t very good at hiding her feelings. She just doesn't have a *poker face*.

2. The businessman kept a *poker face* while he carried out the negotiations. He didn't want to let anyone know how pleased he was with the deal.

The expression originates from the game of poker, in which the players avoid showing any pleasure or displeasure in the cards they have been dealt by keeping an expressionless face.

POP THE QUESTION
to ask someone to get married

1. Jane was hoping Mike would *pop the question* before long. After all, they had been dating each other for more than two years and Jane thought it was time they got married.

2. It came as a complete surprise to Marsha when Bill *popped the question* and asked her to marry him.

The question in the expression is "Will you marry me?" Presumably it is popped because it is supposed to come as a surprise.

POUND OF FLESH
a (figuratively) painful payment of a debt

1. When we fell behind in our mortgage and asked the bank to work out a different payment schedule, they refused and took possession of our house. They got their *pound of flesh*.

2. You've been annoying me for days about the ten dollars I owe you, but I'm afraid I don't have the money right now. You'll have to wait for your *pound of flesh*.

The expression originates from Shakespeare's play *The Merchant of Venice* in which Antonio borrows money from Shylock, the Jewish money lender, promising to pay it back when his ships arrive. When Antonio learns that his ships have sunk at sea, Shylock demands payment in the form of one pound of Antonio's flesh.

PULL (ONESELF) UP BY (ONE'S) BOOTSTRAPS
to improve oneself (usually economically) without help from others

1. Clarence didn't come from a very promising background and no one thought he would succeed. However, he *pulled himself up by his bootstraps*, got a good education, and became a prosperous lawyer.

2. Don't expect other people to help you get ahead in life. If you want to get somewhere, you'll have to *pull yourself up by your bootstraps* and do it for yourself.

PULL OUT ALL THE STOPS
to use everything possible; to spare nothing; to spare no expense

1. They decided to have the best vacation ever, so they flew first-class, took taxis everywhere, stayed in a four-star hotel, and ate at the most expensive restaurants. They *pulled out all the stops*.

2. Our only daughter is getting married. Since it's something that happens only once, we're going to *pull out all the stops*: a big wedding with flowers everywhere and a sit-down dinner for 500 people.

Compare to: *whole hog; whole nine yards; to the hilt; go to town*

The origin of the expression is that in playing an organ, the organist gets the maximum sound from the instrument by pulling out all the stops on the keyboard.

PULL RANK
to take advantage of one's superior position (one's rank)

1. Usually the boss lets all the workers take part in making important decisions, but this time she *pulled rank* and made the decision entirely by herself.

2. First the army officer tried to persuade his men politely to his way of thinking. When they still wouldn't see matters his way, he had to *pull rank* and give them orders.

This phrase is based on one of the meanings of the word *pull*, specifically to exert control.'

PULL SOMEONE'S LEG
to tease, fool, or trick someone in a friendly way

1. You can't believe what John says half the time. I'll bet he was just teasing you. He was just *pulling your leg*.

2. *Stop pulling my leg*! I want you to tell me the truth.

PULL (SOMETHING) OFF
to accomplish something that had appeared difficult to finish or achieve

1. The thieves didn t think they would succeed in stealing the jewels, but they managed to *pull it off*.

2. Do you think we can *pull the deal off*? It's going to take a lot of late nights and hard work to do it.

PULL STRINGS
to use one's influence

1. Can you get me a job in your father's company? I know you can do it if you're willing to *pull strings*.

2. Jane's parents were influential in politics, but she wanted to make her way on her own. She didn t like *pulling strings* to get what she wanted.

The expression originates from the idea of a string puppet or marionette, which can be controlled by pulling on its strings. A person who can pull strings can control a situation and influence others.

PULL THE RUG OUT FROM UNDER (SOMEONE)
to abruptly ruin someone's plans or expectations

1. When Tim went into his supervisor's office, he thought he was going to get a raise for a job well done. He had *the rug pulled out from under* him when the boss fired him instead.

2. Anne pulled *the rug out from under her parents* when she told them that she was not going to medical school and had decided to get married instead.

Compare to: *knock/throw (someone) for a loop*

The expression suggests the feeling of shock a person would have if a rug was literally pulled out from under him or her.

PULL THE WOOL OVER (SOMEONE'S) EYES
to deceive or fool someone

1. The young man was so naive that he believed whatever anyone told him. It was easy to *pull the wool over his eyes*.

2. The children told their mother they were going to school when in fact they planned to go to the movies. They managed *to pull the wool over her eyes*.

Compare to: *song and dance; cock-and-bull story; snow job; fall for (something)*

PULL UP STAKES

to collect one's household belongings and leave one's house or property; to move to another place

1. Life in the big cities of the east was often discouraging, so many families *pulled up stakes* and moved west to California.

2. There aren't many people left in this town. Almost everyone is *pulling up stakes* and moving someplace where they can find a job and make a better living.

This express originated during the 1700s with pioneers moving westward through the United States seeking land to settle on. To claim a portion of land for themselves, the settlers would mark the boundaries of the land with stakes (wood). If they later decided to move and give up claim to the land, they would literally pull up the stakes marking the boundaries. It is often used to describe a sense of abandonment, of leaving one's land behind because one has fallen on hard times.

PUT ALL (ONE'S) EGGS IN ONE BASKET

to invest all one's hopes or plans in only one possible outcome

1. We found a house we want to buy, but we haven't stopped looking at others because the sellers haven't agreed to our price. We don't want to *put all our eggs in one basket*.

2. Sally concentrated all her hopes on going to one particular university. Her parents told her it was a mistake to *put all her eggs in one basket*—that school might not accept her, so she should consider some alternatives.

The expression is usually used in the negative. It suggests that putting all one's eggs in one basket is unwise, because if one drops the basket, all the eggs will break. It would be better to have the eggs divided among several baskets.

PUT (ONE'S) BEST FOOT FORWARD

to try to make the best possible impression

1. Patrick wanted to make a good impression at his job interview, so he dressed carefully and *put his best foot forward*.

2. The teacher asked us to *put our best foot forward* when we met the President. It was such an honor for the school; we wanted the whole school to be proud of us.

PUT (ONE'S) FINGER ON IT

to identify or understand something properly

1. Jim knew there was a problem with the ending of his story, but he couldn't *put his finger on it*. He needed somebody else to point out the problem.

2. Ellie remembered playing the game when she was little, but when she tried to remember how to play, she couldn't *put her finger on it*.

PUT (ONE'S) FOOT DOWN

to be firm and unyielding about something

1. The children were watching more and more television. Finally, their mother *put her foot down* and told them that from then on they could only watch one hour of television a day.

2. I know how much you want a motorcycle, but I just don't think it's safe. I'm going to have to *put my foot down* on this and tell you that you can t have one.

Compare to: *lay down the law; draw the line (at something); read (someone) the riot act*

In this phrase 'put' means to exert control. The expression is often used to describe parents setting rules for their children. The expression is often used in reference to a request, which is refused, or some form of current (bad) behavior that is forbidden.

PUT (ONE'S) MONEY WHERE (ONE'S) MOUTH IS

to support what one is saying by risking or spending money (sentences 1 and 2); to demonstrate in action what one says one can do (sentence 3)

1. The mayor was always talking about doing something good for the homeless people in our city. All we had heard so far was talk, so at the next city council meeting we asked her to *put her money where her mouth was* and actually do something constructive.

2. They talked so much about wanting to help us get a good start in life that I finally said, "Why don't you *put your money where your mouth is?*"

3. Jeffrey talks a lot about how he can drive faster than anyone else in his new sports car, but I wonder if he's willing to *put his money where his mouth is* and actually race against someone.

Compare to: *actions speak louder than words*

The expression is used to challenge someone who talks a lot about doing or being able to do something, but who never actually does anything to demonstrate it.

PUT (SOMEONE) ON THE SPOT

to put someone in a difficult situation or to present someone with a difficult choice; to embarrass someone

1. I knew John had left work to go to the bank when he wasn't supposed to, and the boss *put me on the spot* when he asked if I knew where John was. I didn't want to lie to the boss, but I didn t want to get John in trouble either.

2. Their neighbor *put them on the spot* when she asked to borrow money from them. They liked their neighbor and wanted to stay on good terms with her, but they knew that lending money to a friend frequently leads to disagreement.

Compare to: *over a barrel*

PUT THE CART BEFORE THE HORSE

to reverse the necessary or expected order of two things; to put a later step first

1. Christopher is already making plans to join a law firm next September, but he hasn't even passed the bar exam yet. Isn't he *putting the cart before the horse?*

2. You can't illustrate the book before you have written the text. That's *putting the cart before the horse.*

The expression suggests that one is reversing the natural order of things. The cart must go after the horse in order to get anywhere.

PUT THE SQUEEZE/SCREWS ON/TO

to apply pressure on someone to do something; to force or coerce someone

1. I have two job offers and I haven t been able to decide which one to accept. They are both *putting the squeeze on me* to decide soon.

2. The senator wanted his colleagues to vote for his proposal. They owed him a favor, so he began to *put the screws on.*

3. I'd better pay Jim back soon, or I'm afraid he's going to *put the screws to me.*

R

RACK (ONE'S) BRAIN(S)
to search through one's mind intensively; to try very hard to think of something

1. I've been *racking my brains*, but I just can't remember where I know that person from.
2. When John saw the exam questions, he knew he wasn't prepared. He *racked his brain* for the answers, but he couldn't come up with anything useful.

RAIN ON (SOMEONE'S) PARADE
to spoil someone's happy feelings

1. They're feeling so good today; nothing could *rain on their parade* and spoil the way they feel.
2. I'm in a great mood, so don't tell me anything that might change the way I'm feeling. *Don't rain on my parade.*

Compare to: *wet blanket*

The expression suggests that spoiling someone's happy feelings is similar to having it rain during a parade. The expression is usually used in the negative.

RAINING CATS AND DOGS
to rain very heavily

1. The children should take their raincoats, umbrellas, and boots—it's *raining cats and dogs.*
2. I've never seen such rain! Look how fast it's coming down. It's *raining cats and dogs.*

RAISE CAIN
to cause a disturbance, often because one is extremely angry; to make trouble

1. The citizens were unhappy with the way the city council was running the government. They mounted a protest and *raised Cain* at the next city council meeting to let their feelings be known.
2. Mr. Ward found that his sons had used his tools and left them all over the garage floor. He *raised Cain* when he saw the boys and told them they couldn't use the tools again.
3. Quit *raising Cain!* I know you're angry about the change in our plans, but there is nothing we can do about it.

Compare to: *blow (one's) stack; read (someone) the riot act*

The word *Cain* in the expression refers to a Biblical character, the first son of Adam and Eve, who killed his brother Abel.

RAKE (SOMEONE)/GET RAKED OVER THE COALS
to reprimand or criticize someone harshly

1. The bank teller stood silently in the manager's office while she *raked him over the coals* for the errors he had made that day.

2. The principal discovered who was responsible for the vandalism at the school. He called them into his office and *raked them over the coals.*

Synonyms: *chew (someone) out; read (someone) the riot act*

Compare to: *call (someone) on the carpet; give someone a piece of (one's) mind; lay down the law*

Rake someone over the coals is more severe than *call someone on the carpet.*

RANK AND FILE
the non-management workers in a company or the non-leadership members of a political party

1. The union asked its *rank-and-file* members to vote against the new contract that the company was offering.
2. Ted is getting promoted from the *rank and file* to a position in middle management. He hasn't had much schooling, but his years among the workers have taught him enough to work his way up.

The expression comes from the military formation of soldiers side by side (rank) and one behind the other (file) forming large groups such as platoons. The expression has come to be applied to the non-management workers in a union (sentence 1) or company (sentence 2).

READ BETWEEN THE LINES
to understand a message that is alluded to but not directly said or written

1. Although James didn't say it in so many words, Elizabeth could *read between the lines* that he didn't want to see her again.
2. They tried to give him the bad news gently and without saying it directly, but he didn't seem to understand all their hinting. Finally they asked him, "Can't you *read between the lines?*"

Compare to: *read something into (something)*. The expression suggests that there is meaning hidden between the lines of the words actually written.

READ (SOMEONE) THE RIOT ACT
to reprimand or scold someone harshly

1. When the girls arrived home several hours late, their mother *read them the riot act.*
2. The teacher was very upset that the students rarely turned in their homework or applied themselves to their studies. He *read them the riot act,* telling them that they were foolish not to be making the most of their education.

Compare to: *rake (someone) over the coals; raise Cain; chew (someone) out; call (someone) on the carpet; lay down the law*

The expression originates from the Riot Act of 1716, in which King George I of England decreed that it was unlawful for twelve or more people to assemble in order to protest or act in a 'disruptive' manner. When such an assembly took place, a person of authority was directed to read the Riot Act to the crowd in order to disperse them. Anyone refusing to disperse after the reading could then be arrested.

READ (SOMETHING) INTO (SOMETHING)

to give some meaning to something that is not justified; to imagine some significance that doesn't exist

1. Let me tell you what Scott said to me and then tell me how you would interpret it. Am I *reading more into it* than I should?

2. When the lifeguard passed by and said hello to the young girl, she was convinced that he was in love with her. She was *reading something into* his hello that wasn't there, because he said hello to everyone.

Compare to: *read between the lines*

The expression suggests that one can see meaning in some action or something said or written that is not actually there.

REAL MCCOY, THE

the genuine article; not an imitation or substitute

1. When Mark asked Diana what kind of engagement ring she wanted, she said she didn't want an imitation diamond. She wanted *the real McCoy*.

2. You have to be careful when you go shopping in some places in Europe. Tourists buy a lot of items like watches and purses that supposedly are famous brands, but they aren t *the real McCoy*.

RED HERRING

something used to divert someone's attention from the real or important issue; something used to send a searcher in the wrong direction

1. The newspaper reporters were hot on the trail of a good news story. The man they were pursuing didn't want to be caught, so he tried to mislead them by throwing them *a red herring*.

2. The elected officials in congress don't want the voting public to concentrate on the issue of higher taxes. They divert the public's attention by constantly raising another, less important issue that is nothing more than *a red herring*.

The expression originates from the fact that a red (smoked) herring has a powerful and persistent odor. Centuries ago red herring was used to train dogs to track scents. Those hoping to misdirect tracking dogs would drag red herring across their trails since a dog that gets a whiff of red herring will lose any other scent that it has been following. This expression is often used in the context of mystery stories.

RED-LETTER DAY

an important day; a day to remember

1. Tomorrow is going to be a *red-letter day* for our school. The president is coming to speak to the students and faculty.

2. Mike was made a vice president of the company yesterday. It certainly was a *red-letter day* for him.

The expression originates from the practice of marking holy days in red on some calendars.

RED TAPE

the unnecessary paperwork and procedures of a complicated bureaucracy

1. I try never to ask the government for anything. They are so bogged down in *red tape* that it takes forever, it just isn't worth the effort.

2. When my father was rushed to the hospital, the head nurse cut through all the *red tape* so that he could get to see a doctor immediately.

REST ON (ONE'S) LAURELS

to be so satisfied with what one has already accomplished that one no longer works very hard

1. David had brought a lot of money into the company in the last few months and he deserved to take it easy for a while, but he was working harder than ever. He refused to *rest on his laurels*.

2. Ted invented one new product that was a huge success, but that was over ten years ago. He hasn't produced or contributed much since then—he's been *resting on his laurels*.

RHYME OR REASON, NO

logic; explanation

1. Linda didn't understand why George had done what he did, so she asked him if there was any *rhyme or reason* for his behavior.

2. I was walking quietly down the street when I saw this dog sitting inside its yard. Then, with *no rhyme or reason*, the dog jumped over the fence and bit me.

Compare to: *method in/to (one's) madness*

The expression *rhyme or reason*, which is usually used in the negative or in question form, emphasizes the total lack of apparent rationale for some behavior. The phrase originates from William Shakespeare's play *As You Like It*, in which the character Orlando responds "Neither rhyme nor reason can express how much" when he is asked if he is really as much in love as his rhymes suggest.

RING A BELL

to stir something in one's memory; to cause someone to remember something

1. Laura asked him whether he had heard of Maggie Smith, but he told her that the name didn't *ring a bell*. He couldn't recall whether he had heard of the woman before or not.

2. I'm not sure I'll know any of the guests you're inviting to the party, but if you read the list of names to me, some of them may *ring a bell*.

For centuries bells have been rung to call people's attention or remind them of events, such as bells ringing to announce the start of town meetings, doorbells, and even the ringing of telephone 'bells.'

ROCK THE BOAT

to disturb a situation that is beneficial to the people involved; to cause trouble where none is wanted

1. Unknown to the boss, many employees left work earlier than they were supposed to. They thought they had a good thing going until Bill became angry and *rocked the boat* by telling the boss what was going on.
2. Everyone is happy with the situation as it is. If you change it, you'll be *rocking the boat.*

Compare to: *upset the apple cart*

The expression often describes a situation that becomes worse for the people involved when someone opens the situation to scrutiny. The expression suggests the idea that people who stand up or move about in a boat disturb the other passengers because the boat may capsize. It is frequently used as the negative command, *"Don't rock the boat."*

ROLL OUT THE RED CARPET {THE RED-CARPET TREATMENT}

to give someone the best treatment and show them the finest hospitality

1. The businessmen were given the *red-carpet treatment* by the small town in the hopes that they would decide it was a good place to build a factory.
2. Please don't go to any trouble for us when we come to visit. You don't need to *roll out the red carpet.*

The expression originates from the practice in which, when famous or important people are received, a red carpet is often laid for them to walk on from their carriage or car to the building they will enter. When someone is given the red-carpet treatment, he or she is treated like an extra-special person.

ROLL WITH THE PUNCHES

to adjust to bad fortune; to take a relaxed attitude towards life and its problems

1. Adversity doesn't seem to bother Tom. When something bad happens to him, he *rolls with the punches,* he makes the best of the situation and goes on.
2. In this business there are a lot of unpredictable ups and downs. One has to learn to adjust and take them as they come. One must learn to *roll with the punches.*

Synonym: *take (something) in stride*

Compare to: *go with the flow; like water off a duck's back*

ROSE-COLORED GLASSES, SEE (SOMEONE/SOMETHING) THROUGH

to see something in a falsely good way; not to see something objectively

1. We admit that we've been seeing the situation *through rose-colored glasses,* and now we must face the situation and see it as it really is.

2. Parents almost always have trouble seeing their children the way the rest of the world sees them. Instead, they *look at them through rose-colored glasses.*

The expression suggests that a person looks at something with glasses (eyes) that are not clear. Instead he uses rose (pink)-colored glasses that give a falsely good view of something.

RUB ELBOWS WITH (SOMEONE)

to associate with someone; to come into contact with someone

1. Mr. and Mrs. Campbell go to a lot of fancy dinner parties where they *rub elbows* with some very famous people.
2. In his line of work as a criminal lawyer, Brian *rubs elbows* with some of the lowest levels of society.

This expression refers to the imagery of getting so close to someone that your elbows touch. The term can be used in either a boasting or a negative manner.

RUB (SOMEONE) THE WRONG WAY

to irritate someone

1. Sarah doesn't know what it is about that man, but she just doesn't like him. No matter what he says or does, he *rubs her the wrong way.*
2. I wish I could just ignore Robert's irritating habits, but I can't stand to be around him. He *rubs me the wrong way.*

Compare to: *bug; set (someone's) teeth on edge; get (someone's) dander up; get (someone's) goat*

Whereas *bug, get someone's goat* and *get someone's dander up* can be used to describe a specific irritation or annoyance caused by either someone or something, *rub someone the wrong way* usually describes a clash of personalities that is more general, going beyond a single event or reason.

RULE OF THUMB

a rough guide; an unwritten or customary rule based on experience or practice

1. In this company there is no written rule about how long we can take for our lunch break, but the *rule of thumb* has been about one hour.
2. Sometimes it's hard to know how you are supposed to address people you are meeting for the first time. A good *rule of thumb* is to be formal and wait until they invite you to call them by their first names.

RUN AMOK

to run around in a frenzied or disorderly way

1. I hope the class will walk in an orderly line as we go to the other classroom. There's no need to *run amok.*
2. The boys startled the sheep, and the sheep pushed down the gate to the pen and *ran amok* through the farm.

The expression originates from the Malay word *amuk,* which has a similar meaning.

to outperform someone by a wide margin; to be better than someone

1. Tina is a much better tennis player than Mary. She *ran circles around* Mary in the tennis match yesterday.

2. I'm not very good at math and science. Most people *run circles around me* in those two subjects.

Compare to: *head and shoulders above; not hold a candle to (someone)*

The expression suggests someone who can move quickly around another person, leaving him dazed or sluggishly stuck in the middle. Whereas *run circles around someone* means to outperform someone (usually physically), *head and shoulders above someone* usually refers to a person's character or inner qualities.

to follow a natural progression without interference

1. The doctor told the patient that there was no medicine he could give her for her illness. He told her that she would just have to let the fever *run its course.*

2. There wasn t much the police could do to stop the demonstration. Since it was peaceful, they let the demonstration *run its course.*

The expression is most often used in terms of illness (sentence 1), but can also be used to describe other processes that have a predictable or established course of events.

ordinary or usual

1. That restaurant serves lots of different dishes, but none is outstanding or very much better than in any other restaurant. It's *run-of-the-mill.*

2. Ricky was an average student who liked to play sports as much as the next boy. He was your *run-of-the-mill* student.

The expression *run-of-the-mill* originates from the idea of a product such as fabric, which was first mass-produced (the run) in a mill, enabling it to be uniform.

to belabor something beyond reason; to go too far with something

1. Now that everyone is tired of listening to that idea, why don't you stop talking about it? You have *run it into the ground.*

2. I'm going to push this idea with the boss until he accepts it, even if I have to *run it into the ground.*

Compare to: *beat a dead horse*

Beat a dead horse means to talk about a topic or idea that cannot succeed (it's dead), whereas *run something into the ground* means to talk about a topic or idea that may be viable, but to do so to excess.

S

SACRED COW

an idea or thing that cannot be altered

1. Don't suggest that the boss should get rid of one of his secretaries so that we might hire another clerk. The subject of his secretaries is a *sacred cow*.

2. Even though the country needed to raise more money to pay for military and social programs, the president refused to raise taxes. To him "no new taxes" was a *sacred cow* that he was unwilling to sacrifice.

The expression originates from the Hindu belief that cows are sacred and cannot be killed or eaten. The expression is frequently used to describe an idea or thing that ought to be changed or altered but cannot be because the authority forbids it.

SALES PITCH

a speech or presentation designed to persuade someone to buy or do something

1. I hate door-to-door salespeople. They interrupt whatever you are doing and keep you standing at the door with their *sales pitch* about how good their product is.

2. No one knew how Ken had managed to persuade the boss to give him a bigger office, but they all agreed he must have had a very good *sales pitch*.

Compare to: *(give someone a) snow job; (give someone a) song and dance*

The expression is usually used to describe a sales situation (sentence 1), but it can also be used metaphorically (sentence 2).

SALT OF THE EARTH, THE

a very dependable and unpretentious person

1. You can count on Ruth to be there when you need her. She's *the salt of the earth*.

2. Greg may not be a very exciting person, but he'll never let you down or disappoint you. He's *the salt of the earth*.

SALT (SOMETHING) AWAY

to save, store, or hoard something (usually something highly valued and in danger of being stolen)

1. I don't know what Ann does with all the money she earns, but I know she doesn't spend it on herself. She must be *salting it away* for her retirement.

2. Sometimes we give food to the old man next door, because we know that he doesn't have much money. Whenever we do, we try to give him enough so that he can *salt some of it away* for another day.

Compare to: *on ice; save (something) for a rainy day*

The expression originates from the practice of using salt to preserve food before storing it.

SAVE/LOSE FACE

to maintain/not maintain a degree of pride in a shameful situation

1. The father *lost face* when his son was expelled from school. It was a poor reflection on the man's ability to influence and control his family.

2. I knew that what I had done was wrong, but when I was discovered, I pretended that I hadn't known it was wrong. That way I was able to *save face*.

Originally *lose face* was the direct translation of the Chinese saying tiu lien.'

SAVE (SOMETHING) FOR A RAINY DAY

to save something, usually money, for a possible future need

1. Rob saves a portion of every paycheck in the bank. He's not saving for anything in particular, but one never knows when one might need some extra money all of a sudden. He's *saving for a rainy day*.

2. My mother always made me save some of my money in case I needed some unexpectedly. She made me *save for a rainy day*.

Compare to: *salt (something) away; on ice*

The expression suggests that a rainy day is one when a person will not be able to earn any money, and so he or she needs to prepare for such a day by setting aside some money now.

SAY A MOUTHFUL

to say something of a significant or shocking nature (sentence 1); to say more than one should (sentence 2)

1. John pushed his way in to the party and confronted Laura. He began to rant and rave and say things everyone knew he would later regret. He *said a mouthful*.

2. Everybody managed to keep the surprise party a secret until the last minute, when Jennifer's younger sister gave it away. She *said a mouthful* before she remembered that the party was supposed to be a secret.

Compare to: *go off half-cocked*

The expression is usually used to describe when someone says a lot, not so much in terms of the number of words as in the significance of the words.

SCARED OUT OF (ONE'S) WITS

so afraid that one is unable to think clearly

1. You shouldn't jump out of the shadows like that! You *scared me out of my wits!*

2. Michelle's brother played a prank on her, but she didn't think it was funny. She was *scared out of her wits.*

This expression is usually used as an exaggeration to mean "very frightened for a short time."

SCREW LOOSE/LOOSE SCREW, HAVE A

to be harmlessly crazy

1. Sometimes Mr. Simpson talks to himself, and sometimes he imagines that he sees creatures from outer space. I think he *has a screw loose.*

2. The old lady on the bench will tell you the story of her life if you give her a chance. I imagine she's just lonely or she *has a loose screw* somewhere.

Compare to: *bats in (one's) belfry; out to lunch; off (one's) rocker*

SECOND-GUESS

to dispute or try to understand someone's reason for doing something

1. No one knows for sure why the boss quit so abruptly, but we are all trying to *second-guess* his reasons.

2. Peggy came to work and simply announced that she was leaving her husband. She offered no explanation and told everyone who asked that it was none of their business. She told everyone not to *second-guess* why she left her husband.

SECOND-RATE

of inferior quality; not the best

1. This hotel isn't the best. It's really a *second-rate* place.

2. When they remodeled their kitchen, they bought all new appliances of the best quality. They wanted nothing that was *second-rate.*

Synonyms: *third-rate; fourth-rate*

Antonym: *first-rate*

Expressions using *rate* generally go only as far as *fourth-rate*. *Second-, third-,* and *fourth-rate* are synonymous. There are no degrees of inferiority. They are all opposites of *first-rate*.

SECOND THOUGHTS, HAVE

to begin to have doubts; to question and re-examine a decision

1. After you have decided to get married, it's not unusual to have *second thoughts* and wonder whether you are really ready for such a big step.

2. I know we've already made the commitment to buy that house, but now I'm having *second thoughts* about it. Are you sure it was a wise decision?

Compare to: *cold feet*

Whereas *get cold feet* means to change one's mind because of doubts, *have second thoughts* means only to begin to have doubts. One may or may not change one's mind based on *second thoughts.*

SEE EYE TO EYE

to agree

1. It's relatively unusual for teenagers and their parents to *see eye to eye* on some issues like driving privileges, dating, and the importance of school.

2. The two firms broke off their partnership because they no longer *saw eye to eye* on how much money to invest in new research and development.

SEE RED

to get angry

1. John *saw red* when his boss tried to make everyone in the office believe that John had made the mistake.

2. My father *sees red* when I come home late.

Compare to: *fly off the handle; blow (one's) stack; lose (one's) temper*

The expression probably originates from the idea that a bull is supposed to become enraged when it sees the bullfighter's red cape.

SEE (SOMETHING) THROUGH

to finish something one has started

1. The boy had said he would do the job, but it was more work than he had expected. However, he decided to *see the job through* because it was the right thing to do.

2. It wasn't a pleasant task, but Jane knew she had to finish it. She *saw it through* to the end.

Compare to: *see through (something/someone)*

SEE THE LIGHT

to understand something clearly

1. Wendy was completely fooled by the young man. We all wondered when she would *see the light.*

2. They finally *saw the light* when we explained the situation to them.

Compare to: *dawn on (someone)*

Dawn on someone means to understand something some time after it should have become apparent, whereas *see the light* simply means to understand.

SEE THROUGH (SOMETHING/SOMEONE)

to not be fooled by a false front or disguise that someone presents in order to mislead; to understand the true nature of someone or something

1. The little boy told his mother that he was not the one who had taken the candy, but his mother *saw through his story* because she could see chocolate on his face.

2. The pair had everyone convinced they were a luckless but well-intentioned couple. Very few people could *see through them*, and many gave them money, food, and clothing.

Compare to: *see (something) through*

SEE WHICH WAY THE WIND BLOWS

to determine what stance to take based on what others want, even though such actions or words may not be what one sincerely wants to do or say

1. Many politicians try to say what they think their constituents want to hear, even though they don't always mean it. The politicians look to *see which way the wind blows* before they speak.

2. Fred has learned to survive in his job by bending to the will and desires of each boss he has had. He *sees which way the wind blows* and changes his behavior accordingly.

The expression is often used in reference to a political or diplomatic situation. It has the negative connotation of being opportunistic.

SELL LIKE HOTCAKES

to sell quickly

1. When the idea of a photocopying machine first became popular, the machines *sold like hotcakes*.

2. The man who ran the snack bar hoped that the weather on the day of the parade would be hot, because then his ice cream would *sell like hotcakes*.

Compare to: *take off*

Hotcake is another word for pancake.

SELL (SOMEONE) A BILL OF GOODS [SOLD A BILL OF GOODS]

to sell someone something that is worthless (sentence 1), or to make someone believe something that is untrue (sentence 2); to deceive someone

1. The ring looked real on television, but when it arrived in the mail, Paula knew she had been *sold a bill of goods*.

2. The project manager told us that construction would be finished by August; it wasn't until later that we discovered he had *sold us a bill of goods*.

SET (SOMEONE'S) TEETH ON EDGE

to irritate

1. I wish you wouldn't talk during the movie. The noise really *sets my teeth on edge*.

2. That woman always pretends like she's giving me a compliment, but I think she's insulting me. It *sets my teeth on edge*.

Synonyms: *rub (someone) the wrong way, get (someone's) dander/hackles up, get (someone's) goat, bug*

SEVENTH HEAVEN, IN

blissfully happy

1. Cindy met Roger three weeks ago and fell madly in love with him. She's been *in seventh heaven* ever since.

2. We've been *in seventh heaven* knowing that we're going to have a baby.

Synonyms: *on cloud nine; walking on air*

SHAKE A LEG

to hurry

1. Come on, Sam, we don't have all day. Hurry up! *Shake a leg!*

2. I asked you ten minutes ago to stop playing and clean up this mess. We have to go in five minutes. You kids had better *shake a leg*.

Synonyms: *Step on it!; Get a move on!*

Antonyms: *hold (one's) horses; keep (one's) shirt on*

The expression is never used in the past tense form "shook," but it can be used in the future tense.

SHIPS PASSING IN THE NIGHT

two people whose lives come together or whose paths cross for a short time

1. Dan met the woman of his dreams, but he wasn't quite ready to get married. They dated for a while and then went their separate ways. They were *ships passing in the night*.

2. I came to this city in 1985 and left shortly after I met Robert. Our lives touched only briefly. We were *ships passing in the night*.

The expression is frequently used to describe a romance that is not meant to be because it is the wrong time or the wrong place.

SHOOT THE BREEZE

to chat or to pass time by chatting; to talk idly

1. During our lunch hour, we like to sit around and *shoot the breeze*. We talk about all kinds of things and nothing in particular.

2. I sometimes wonder if government employees ever work. They seem to sit around all day talking to each other. They always seem to be just *shooting the breeze*.

Shoot the breeze often includes the idea of chatting because one has some time to "kill" or is waiting for some amount of time to pass.

SHOT IN THE ARM

something that stimulates, boosts, or renews people's interest

1. The exciting and innovative programs introduced by the new manager were a real *shot in the arm*. Everyone became motivated to make them work.

2. The new president stimulated the citizens to take a greater interest in the welfare of the country. He was a *shot in the arm* for a nation that had become apathetic and indifferent.

The expression originates from the idea of a hypodermic injection to make a sick person feel better.

SHOT IN THE DARK
a guess, often wild or based on little information

1. Charles didn't really know the reason why his son was in a bad mood, but he guessed that perhaps he had gotten some bad grades. Charles's guess was a *shot in the dark*.

2. I don't know what they would like for a wedding gift, but we could take a *shot in the dark* and get them something for the kitchen.

The expression suggests that the probability of a correct guess is as small as the probability of hitting something that one shoots at in the dark.

SIT TIGHT
to wait quietly and patiently, often in an anxious situation

1. The stock market was falling sharply, but Lucy didn't panic and sell her stocks. Instead she *sat tight* and waited for the market to rise again.

2. Margie called late at night to tell us that her car had broken down and to ask us to come and pick her up. We told her to *sit tight* and we would be there as soon as possible.

Synonym: *keep (one's) cool*.

The expression *sit tight* is often used in situations of danger or panic or in situations where a calm, cool head is needed. It always uses the adjective "tight" rather than the grammatically correct "tightly".

SITTING PRETTY
in a good or advantageous situation; living comfortably

1. John had managed to work his way into a position of power and influence. He was certainly *sitting pretty* until it was discovered that he was stealing money from the company and was fired.

2. I'm going to be careful how I spend and save my money now, so that when I retire I'll be *sitting pretty* and won't have to worry about my finances.

The expression is often used to describe a financially advantageous situation (sentence 2). It is always used in the present participle form. It can be used in the past or future tenses by making the verb be past (sentence 1) or future (sentence 2).

SIXTH SENSE
a feeling, intuition or premonition not based on one of the five senses: sight, hearing, taste, touch, or smell

1. Carrie has an uncanny sense of what's going to happen in the future. It's almost as though she has a *sixth sense*.

2. They had a terrible feeling that something bad had happened to their son. They had no rational reason for thinking it; it was just a *sixth sense*.

The expression originates from the idea that, whereas everyone is born with the five senses of sight, hearing, taste, touch, and smell, some people seem to have an additional sense that enables them to perceive events or things that others cannot.

SKELETON IN THE CLOSET {FAMILY SKELETON}
an event in one's past or family that is embarrassing and that one would prefer to keep secret

1. Before I took this job with the government, I had to reveal the fact that I had been arrested when I was a teenager. That has always been my *skeleton in the closet*.

2. Rachel's family had a relative who spent years in prison. They always tried to keep that *family skeleton* a secret.

The expression suggests something undesirable that is hidden away in the closet but that one cannot get rid of.

SLEEP LIKE A LOG/ROCK
to sleep so soundly that noise doesn't wake the person

1. Steve had to have two alarm clocks set to wake him up because one was never loud enough. He *slept like a log*.

2. As a rule, the baby never wakes up during the night. She *sleeps like a rock*, and even the noise of the TV doesn't wake her.

The expression suggests that it is as difficult to wake such a person as it would be to wake a log or a rock.

SLIP THROUGH (SOMEONE'S) FINGERS, LET (SOMEONE/SOMETHING)
to lose something because one takes too much time to consider the situation

1. They had the opportunity to make a lot of money, but they didn't act quickly enough and the chance *slipped through their fingers*.

2. When Mike asked Irene to marry him, she told him she wanted time to think it over. But she waited too long and Mike married someone else. She *let him slip through her fingers*.

Synonym: *miss the boat*

The expression suggests that the thing or person one wants to keep is slippery or hard to hold on to, like water or sand. Despite the fact that one tries to grasp it, it disappears between one's fingers.

SLOW BURN
to be quietly angry

1. Jack didn t get promoted to a new job and, although he hasn't said anything about it, I know he's doing a *slow burn*.

2. I do a *slow burn* every time my husband expects me to look after the children while he plays golf with his friends.

SLOW/QUICK OFF THE MARK
slow [or quick] to understand a situation

1. Keith never got a chance to play in the school marching band because he was *slow off the mark* and didn't sign up for it by the deadline.

2. Katherine succeeds at whatever she attempts because she's very much aware of what's going on around her. She's *quick off the mark*.

The expression suggests a race in which the participants are slow [or quick] to leave the point of departure (the mark).

SNOWBALL'S CHANCE IN HELL
no chance at all

1. Kay has a *snowball's chance in hell* of getting into that college. She has bad grades and poor exam scores.

2. They don't have a *snowball's chance in hell* of raising enough money to send him on that trip, because they don't have anything worth selling.

The expression suggests that the likelihood of something happening is as small as the probability that a snowball will not melt in the fires of hell.

SOMETHING TO CROW ABOUT
an exceptional accomplishment; an achievement that is worth bragging about

1. We're really proud of Janie. She got an outstanding score on her entrance exams. It really is *something to crow about*.

2. If you let Bill win, he'll never let us hear the end of it. You'll just be giving him *something to crow about*.

Synonym: *feather in (one's) cap*

Antonym: *nothing to write home about*

The expression suggests the sound a rooster makes to draw attention to itself.

SOUR GRAPES
a situation where a person criticizes something or someone out of jealousy

1. When Nicolas found out that he wasn't going to be promoted, he told people that he hadn't really wanted to stay with the company anyway. It was a case of *sour grapes*.

2. I know this sounds like *sour grapes,* but I'm just as glad that I didn't get into college. I think I'd rather get a job.

The expression originates from Aesop's fable about a fox that wanted some grapes from a vine but was unable to jump high enough to get them. In disgust, he claimed that they weren't worth having anyway because they were probably sour.

SOW (ONE'S) WILD OATS
to do foolish or wild things, usually as a youth

1. You would never know it, but their father was quite a troublemaker in his youth. He *sowed his wild oats* before he became a family man and an important member of the community.

2. Nancy doesn't want to settle down to a family and career until she has spent a few years traveling, having a good time, and *sowing her wild oats*.

The expression has traditionally been used to describe the behavior of a young man (sentence 1), although nowadays it can be used to describe young people of both sexes.

SPEAK OF THE DEVIL
an expression used when someone who is being talked about has just appeared

1. Jan brought up the subject of Tom at the meeting when, all of a sudden, he walked in. *"Speak of the devil!"* said Jan. "We were just talking about you."

2. "Where's Ernie?" I asked, just as Ernie came through the door. "Here I am," said Ernie. *"Speak of the devil,"* I said.

The expression has a slightly negative connotation, because of the reference to the devil, but it is usually meant humorously.

SPEAK (ONE'S) MIND
to tell someone how one feels or what one thinks

1. Donald wondered if he could *speak his mind* freely, but decided it would be best if he kept his opinions to himself. So he didn t tell her what he really thought about her.

2. I've always been honest and open with you about how I feel and what I think. I've never been shy about *speaking my mind*.

Synonym: *speak (one's) piece*

SPEAK (ONE'S) PIECE

to tell someone how one feels or what one thinks

1. Pam's father was unhappy that she intended to marry a man he didn't approve of. He wanted her to know why he disapproved of the man, so he *spoke his piece,* but he ended by saying that he would leave the decision up to her.

2. I've always been honest with you about how I feel and what I think. I've never been shy about *speaking my piece.*

Synonym: *speak (one's) mind*

The expression *speak one's piece* is usually used to describe what someone does when he disagrees strongly with someone else but has little control over the situation. The speaker wants the person to know his feelings and may present them in an uninterrupted monologue (piece).

SPILL THE BEANS

to reveal a secret

1. I told Bob not to tell anyone my secret, but he couldn't keep his mouth shut. He *spilled the beans* to the first person who walked through the door.

2. The boss was annoyed when he learned that we all knew he planned to quit. He wanted to know who had *spilled the beans.*

Synonym: *let the cat out of the bag*

Antonym: *keep (something) under (one's) hat*

SPITTING IMAGE

an exact likeness

1. Although Roger doesn't look very much like his father or mother, his grandmother says he's the *spitting image* of her late husband, Roger's grandfather.

2. The girls in that family have their mother's mouth, nose and eyes. They are the *spit and image* of their mother.

Compare to: *chip off the old block*

Spitting image refers to a physical likeness, whereas *a chip off the old block* refers to a likeness in character or personality. The expression is usually used to describe a child's resemblance to a family member.

SPLIT HAIRS

to argue about some detail that is not important

1. The girl's mother asked what time they got home and the girl told her 10:00. The brother insisted that it was 10:05. The girl told him he was *splitting hairs* and that five minutes didn't really make a difference.

2. We can't seem to agree on this minor point, but I don t think it's worth arguing about. I'm not going to *split hairs* with you about this.

The expression suggests that a hair is so thin that it would be pointless to try to split it. Similarly, it is pointless to argue over details of no consequence.

SPRING (SOMETHING) ON (SOMEONE)

to surprise someone with something

1. Grace thought she had done well on the test, so it came as a shock when she discovered that she'd failed. The teacher *sprang it on her* very suddenly.

2. You have to prepare Mark for surprises or bad news that he's not expecting. Don't *spring anything on him.*

Synonym: *knock/throw (someone) for a loop*

The expression is usually used to describe surprising someone with some unexpected news.

SPUR OF THE MOMENT, ON THE

suddenly or spontaneously; without advance planning

1. They didn't have plans for the weekend, but *on the spur of the moment*, they decided to take a trip to the beach.

2. Betsy isn't a very spontaneous person. She can't just do something *on the spur of the moment.*

3. I didn't really plan to go out last night. It was a *spur-of-the-moment* decision.

Synonym: *off the cuff*

SQUARE DEAL

a fair arrangement, fair treatment, or a fair price

1. We bought our car from the dealership in town, and they gave us a good car at a fair price. It was a *square deal.*

2. The management of this company are always out to get what they can from the workers without fair treatment or compensation. They have never given anyone a *square deal.*

Synonym: *fair and square*

In this expression, *square* means *right.*

SQUARE MEAL

full and well-balanced meal

1. That man is so thin and gaunt. He looks like he hasn t had a *square meal* in weeks.

2. The children's doctor recommends that they eat three *square meals* a day. Each meal should include a vegetable or fruit, milk or cheese, meat or some form of protein, and rice or bread.

STAND (ONE'S) GROUND

to be firm in one's resolve or not to alter one's position (sentence 1); not to give up any territory (sentence 2)

1. The union workers will not give in to the demands of the factory management. They want better wages, better health benefits and improved working conditions, and they're going to *stand their ground.*

2. When the goose was threatened by the approaching fox, she *stood her ground* and hissed and pecked at him. She would protect her baby goslings at all costs.

Antonyms: *give in; knuckle under*

Compare to: *stick to (one's) guns*

Stick to one's guns more narrowly means to be firm in one's resolve, and could be used in sentence 1 but not in sentence 2. The expression *stand one's ground* suggests having one's feet firmly planted on the ground and not giving up any ground to one's adversary. It is often used to describe the behavior of a wild animal that is being threatened by its enemy.

STAND ON (ONE'S) OWN TWO FEET
to be independent and self-supporting

1. They told their twenty-year-old son that it was time he found a job and began to support himself. It was time for him to *stand on his own two feet*.

2. I was so glad to hear that Pete and Gloria got a house of their own and that they no longer have to live with her parents. They are finally *standing on their own two feet*.

The expression suggests that when a person uses his own two feet, he is not relying on others for support. The expression always calls for two feet even when the subject is plural (sentence 2) and four feet would be more logical.

STAND OUT IN A/THE CROWD
to be distinguishable from others in a group; distinctive

1. Dianne has her own style and rarely follows current fashion. If you saw her on the street, she would *stand out in a crowd*.

2. Paul does what everyone else does and goes along with what other people think and say. He doesn't like to *stand out in the crowd*.

Compare to: *stick out like a sore thumb*

Whereas *stand out in a crowd* is usually a positive attribute, *stick out like a sore thumb* is a negative one. The expression *stand out in a crowd* suggests a degree of distinctiveness and independence.

START (SOMETHING) FROM SCRATCH
to start from the very beginning; to start from the very first step

1. The laboratory experiment failed for some unknown reason, so the chemist decided to *start the experiment from scratch*. He started over completely with new bottles of chemicals and new equipment.

2. Karen had to throw out what she had already done. She wasn't able to save any of it. She had to *start from scratch*.

Compare to: *back to square one; make (something) from scratch*

STEP ON IT
to hurry

1. Mother was late for a doctor's appointment and the children were slow getting into the car. "*Step on it!*" she snapped. "We're late."

2. As the ambulance left for the hospital with my sick father in the back, I asked the ambulance driver to *step on it*. I wanted him to waste no time getting to the hospital.

Synonyms: *shake a leg; get a move on*

Antonyms: *hold (one's) horses; keep (one's) shirt on*

The expression is often used when the speaker is annoyed or short-tempered, as in sentence 1, and probably stems from the idea of pressing down hard on the gas pedal to make a car go faster.

STEW IN (ONE'S) OWN JUICES
to suffer the consequences of one's own actions

1. The boss is annoyed that we haven't finished this report yet, but he really didn t give us enough time to do it. He's in the office pacing the floor, but I'm not going to work any faster. Let him *stew in his own juices* for a while.

2. You brought this bad situation on yourself, and no one is going to go out of his way to rescue you. You'll just have to *stew in your own juices*.

The expression suggests that one is "cooked" (stewed) in one's own unpleasant but self-made situation.

STICK-IN-THE-MUD
someone who is seen as never wanting to take part in fun activities

1. Let's go to the beach. You don t want to sit around the house all day, do you? Don t be such a *stick-in-the-mud*!

2. Everyone thought Herman was a *stick-in-the-mud* because he never liked to do anything interesting or exciting. He never took part in the tricks that the other students played on each other or on their teachers.

Compare to: *wet blanket*

The expression *stick-in-the-mud* is derogatory. It is usually said to taunt someone who is less daring, less spontaneous, or more conservative than others. It suggests the slow or sluggish movement of something stuck in mud.

STICK (ONE'S) NECK OUT
to take a risk

1. Larry helped me when no one else would, and I would do the same for him. I don t mind *sticking my neck out* for a friend like him.

2. Jack was too scared to *stick his neck out* and stand with the rest of the workers in their demands for better working conditions. He was afraid he would lose his job.

Synonym: *go out on a limb*

The expression suggests that sticking one's neck out may lead to having one's head chopped off.

STICK (ONE'S) NOSE IN

to try to find out about someone else's private business

1. Don't *stick your nose in* where it's not wanted. This matter is between Pat and me, and it has nothing to do with you.

2. I mind my own business, and don't get involved in other people's personal affairs. I don't *stick my nose in* where it doesn't belong.

Antonym: *mind (one's) own business*

The expression *stick one's nose in* has a negative connotation.

STICK OUT LIKE A SORE THUMB

not to blend in; to be obvious and prominent or easily seen

1. John said he planned to wear shorts and a sweatshirt to the wedding, but I told him it would be completely inappropriate. I told him he would *stick out like a sore* thumb and everyone would notice him.

2. The paintings of the modern artists *stuck out like a sore thumb* in the classical art museum. They just didn't belong there, grouped together with the old masters.

Compare to: *stand out in a crowd*

Whereas *stand out in a crowd* is usually a positive attribute, *stick out like a sore thumb* is a negative one. It is used to describe someone (or, less frequently, something) in a situation where one ought to blend in but doesn't.

STICK TO (ONE'S) GUNS

to be firm in one's resolve or not to alter one's position

1. Peggy was determined to ask her boss for a pay raise, but when she raised the issue, she let the boss talk her out of it. She didn't *stick to her guns*.

2. Little children often test their parents to see how much they can get away with. It's important for parents to *stick to their guns* when their children try to get something undeserved out of them.

Antonyms: *give in; knuckle under*

Compare to: *stand (one's) ground*

Stand one's ground can also include the idea of being firm against one's enemy. It could be substituted in each sentence above to suggest a more adversarial relationship.

STONEWALL

to avoid answering a question directly by being deliberately vague about it, or by talking a lot but not saying anything meaningful

1. The newspaper reporter asked the president whether he intended to seek reelection. The president did not want to reveal his decision, so he *stonewalled* by talking around it.

2. The bank manager was called before the board of directors to answer questions about the large number of bad loans made by his bank. The directors asked him who had approved the loans. The manager said he wasn't sure, that the decisions were made by several people and it would be hard to determine who specifically had approved each one. The manager was *stonewalling* the board.

Compare to: *beat around the bush; hem and haw*

Hem and haw describes being at a loss for words, making only meaningless sounds, whereas *stonewall* means talking but saying little of substance. The expression is usually used to describe people that want to avoid taking responsibility or answering a direct question.

STRAIGHT AND NARROW

the path of correct social or ethical behavior that society approves of

1. Ruth never does anything surprising or slightly out of the ordinary. She follows the *straight and narrow*.

2. The boss always follows the *straight and narrow, so* we know he will treat us fairly and honestly.

Compare to: *toe the line*

STRAIGHT FROM THE HORSE'S MOUTH

directly from the primary source; directly from the person or people involved

1. You may not believe this, but the boss is quitting the company. The boss told me himself. I heard it *straight from the horse's mouth*.

2. Tim asked Molly where she heard the news. He thought perhaps it was just a rumor, but Molly said she got it *straight from the horse's mouth*.

Antonym: *hear (something) through the grapevine*

The expression is used to describe the source of information, usually of a rumor or of something that is not likely to be believed. The origin of the expression is the fact that one can always tell the true age of a horse from an examination of its teeth, i.e. from its mouth. Thus, the horse's mouth is the most authoritative source of information about its age.

STRANGE BEDFELLOWS

people or things that one does not normally expect to find together

1. I never thought I'd see two politicians from opposite ends of the political spectrum working together to pass the same law. They certainly are *strange bedfellows*.

2. John and Charlie rarely have the same opinion about anything, so it was surprising to find them agreeing on such a controversial issue. Aren't they *strange bedfellows?*

STRAPPED FOR CASH

not having quite enough money

1. I'd love to have dinner with you, but I'm *strapped for cash* and can't afford a restaurant. Maybe we can eat at home.
2. Martha got tired of being *strapped for cash*, so she made a budget and didn't use more money than she could afford.

STRAW THAT BROKE THE CAMEL'S BACK, THE

the final thing or action which is too much or goes too far

1. Constance finally quit her job because the situation was becoming intolerable. The boss asked her to make the coffee and act as a hostess even though she was hired as an accountant. The *straw that broke the camel's back* came when the boss asked her to go out and buy his family's Christmas presents and then complained because she couldn't get her work done.
2. First the builder dropped paint on their new carpet. Then he backed his ladder through their window. They told him to get out and not come back when he backed his truck over their prized flowerbed. That was *the straw that broke the camel's back.*

Synonym: *last/final straw*

Both expressions suggest the idea of loading straw (a relatively light material) onto a camel's back until one more light straw (the last straw) breaks the camel's back.

STREET SMARTS

the knowledge one needs to live on the streets; less literally, it means knowledge of the way things work in the real world

1. Jim and George drifted from city to city, living off the streets and stealing. They managed to avoid getting caught by the police because of their *street smarts.*
2. Ms. Howard is a good businesswoman. Although she studied at Harvard Business School, she's also picked up some *street smarts* and can play hardball when she has to.

STRETCH THE TRUTH

to be truthful technically, but to distort the truth so that others are led to believe something that is not true

1. When people asked Peter if he was a manager, he *stretched the truth* by telling them that he managed the office where he worked. What he didn t tell them was that he was the only person in his office and he only managed himself.

2. Sometimes when people apply for a job, they *stretch the truth* about what they did in their previous jobs in order to make themselves seem more important or more desirable.

Compare to: *white lie*

The expression suggests that one can distort or bend the truth, so that others are misled, without actually telling a lie.

STRIKE IT RICH

to make money (sentence 1); or, less literally, to be wildly successful (sentence 2)

1. Calvin was very talented when it came to business and finance, and it was only natural that he would *strike it rich* when he invested in the stock market on Wall Street.
2. Carol was just trying to get a photograph of the actor, but she *struck it rich* when he asked her if she wanted an exclusive interview, too.

Synonym: *hit pay dirt, hit the jackpot*

The expression originated with the idea of miners discovering precious minerals, but it is also used as a metaphor to describe finding anything of value.

STRING (SOMEONE) ALONG

to make someone believe something that is not true

1. Mark had no scruples when it came to romance. He would *string some poor girl along* until he found someone he liked better. Then he would drop the first girl without a second thought and leave her broken-hearted.
2. The crook *strung the old lady along* with the story that he was investing her money in something safe, when in fact he was stealing from her.

The expression is often used to describe what a false-hearted lover does to someone who is naive or unsuspecting (sentence 1).

STUFFED SHIRT

a man who is tiresome, pompous and self-important

1. Stanley is a bit of a *stuffed shirt*. He's arrogant and pompous and he tries to make everyone else think he's so important.
2. We hate going to those business conventions. It's just a bunch of *stuffed shirts,* sitting around trying to impress each other.

Compare to: *old fuddy-duddy*

Describing someone as *a stuffed* shirt is clearly disparaging, whereas *old fuddy-duddy* describes someone who is a harmlessly and often humorously old-fashioned person. The expression *stuffed shirt* is always used to describe a man, never a woman.

SUIT/FIT (SOMEONE/SOMETHING) TO A T

perfectly; exactly

1. Margie tried on the dress in the store and looked at herself in the mirror. The dress *suited her to a T*.

2. The carpenter removed the old window and put in the replacement. It *fit the space to a T*.

SWALLOW (ONE'S) PRIDE

to accept something humiliating

1. My aunt is a stubborn woman. She would rather lose everything than *swallow her pride* and take money or help from us.

2. There's nothing to be ashamed of in being able to *swallow your pride* and admit when you are wrong. In fact, it's a sign of maturity.

Compare to: *eat crow; eat humble pie*

SWEAT BLOOD

to put out a great deal of effort; to work very, very hard

1. Gary had to work day and night to keep his large family in food and clothing. He *sweat blood* for them.

2. There's no point in *sweating blood* for some people. They'll never be happy no matter how hard you try.

The expression suggests that one works so hard that one sweats blood, a fluid more vital than perspiration.

SWEEP (SOMEONE) OFF HIS/HER FEET

to overwhelm someone, often causing him or her to fall in love

1. Marcella was an impressionable young woman with little experience of romance. Richard just *swept her off her feet* when he started to date her.

2. Judy and Joe went to Hawaii on the holiday vacation of their dreams. They were *swept off their feet* by the warm and friendly atmosphere.

Compare to: *head over heels in love*

One can be *swept off one's feet* by either a person (sentence 1) or a place or situation (sentence 2).

T

TAKE A SHINE/FANCY TO (SOMEONE/SOMETHING)

to like someone spontaneously

1. Tom liked Kate from the moment he met her. He *took a shine to her* instantly.

2. They decided to buy the house without much discussion because they *took a fancy to it*.

Compare to: *tickle (someone's) fancy*

TAKE/GIVE (SOMEONE) A RAIN CHECK

to accept a different time for an appointment from the original one; to request that an appointment be rescheduled

1. Thanks for asking me to have lunch with you today. Unfortunately, I'm busy. Can I *take a rain check?* I'm free for lunch almost any day next week.

2. Bonnie had a date with Tom for Saturday but her mother became ill and she told him she couldn't make it. She asked if he could *give her a rain check* for another time.

The expression originates from baseball and other outdoor sporting events, in which rain checks are given if the game is canceled because of rain. The *rain check* entitles the spectator to see another game on another day free of charge.

TAKE IT EASY

to relax

1. Don't get so upset over something that doesn't matter. *Take it easy.*

2. Roger had a heart attack last year. Now he *takes it easy* and doesn't work as hard as he used to.

TAKE OFF

to leave quickly (sentence 1) or to do well in sales (sentences 2 and 3)

1. The boys threw rocks at the old man's windows. When he came out of the house to chase them away, *they took off*.

2. The young man invented a gadget to use in the kitchen and now he is trying to sell it. It hasn't sold well so far but he's sure that eventually it will *take off*.

Synonym: *sell like hotcakes* (sentence 2)

TAKE POTLUCK

to accept whatever is available

1. I know it's short notice but you're welcome to join us for dinner if you don't mind *taking potluck*.

2. There isn t much choice left, but I'm not picky. I'm happy to *take potluck*.

The expression probably originates from the idea of a potluck dinner, where each guest brings one different food or dish to contribute to everyone's meal. Nobody knows in advance exactly what foods will be brought. Potluck dinners and potluck picnics are popular in the U.S. They are informal gatherings and easy to organize because no one person has to provide more than one dish.

TAKE (SOMEONE) TO THE CLEANERS

to steal or cheat someone out of all of his or her money

1. The unsuspecting woman agreed to invest all her money with an unethical investment banker. He *took her to the cleaners*, and she was left without a penny to her name.

2. I made the mistake of giving my dishonest nephew a blank check from my bank account. Instead of writing it for the amount we had agreed on, he wrote it for every cent I had. He *took me to the cleaners*.

Synonym: *clean (someone) out*

TAKE (SOMETHING) IN STRIDE

to accept and adjust to bad fortune or trouble

1. When I told them the bad news, I expected them to be upset, but they *took it in stride*. It didn't seem to bother them at all.

2. Rebecca isn't bothered by unexpected surprises. She always *takes things in stride*.

Synonym: *roll with the punches*

Similar to: *like water off a duck's back*

The expression *take something in stride* suggests that when one is confronted by something unexpected, it does not interrupt one's stride (i.e., the way one walks).

TAKE (SOMETHING) WITH A GRAIN OF SALT

to be skeptical or cautious about believing a story or an explanation

1. You can't believe everything Peggy says. She's inclined to exaggerate, so you have to *take what she says with a grain of salt*.

2. Nick is just making things sound worse than they really are. *Take it with a grain of salt*.

TAKE (SOMETHING) BY STORM

to overwhelm someone or something, often by becoming famous quickly (sentence 1), or by spreading very rapidly (sentence 2)

1. The Beatles were rock musicians who *took the world by storm* in the 1960s.

2. Fear of the disease spread across the country very quickly. Panic *took the nation by storm*.

TAKE THE BULL BY THE HORNS

to take action in a difficult or unpleasant situation

1. When it came time to paint the living room, nobody knew where to start. Ben *took the bull by the horns*, chose a brush, and started painting, and everybody followed his lead.

2. You know what you want to do for a living, but you need to start working toward your goal. Don't be afraid to *take the bull by the horns* and start applying for jobs.

Compare to: *bite the bullet; face the music; grin and bear it*

The expression *take the bull by the horns* does not suggest that the person is necessarily responsible for the difficult situation in the same way that to *face the music* does.

TAKE THE CAKE

to outdo; to exceed normal behavior; metaphorically, to win the prize

1. David has done foolish things in the past, but I never thought he would do anything this foolish. This really *takes the cake*.

2. They have always used poor judgment when it comes to social affairs, but this outdoes anything they have done in the past. This time, their behavior *takes the cake*.

The expression is often used to express one's shock at impolite or bad behavior. The shocking behavior is usually something that surpasses some previous bad behavior. It is usually used in the present simple tense and infrequently in the past tense.

TAKE THE WIND OUT OF (SOMEONE'S) SAILS

to deflate someone's ego (sentence 1) or to ruin or destroy someone's high expectations (sentence *2*)

1. Mary was so sure that she was going to be offered that job. Wait until I tell her that the position has been given to Roger instead. That'll *take the wind out of her sails*

2. I was hoping to be accepted by that university. When the rejection letter arrived, it really *took the wind out of my sails*.

The expression probably originates from the sport of racing sailboats. When one sailboat cuts in front of another, it literally *takes the wind out of* the rear boat's sails, causing it to lose its speed. The expression can be used to describe one's own disappointment (sentence 2) or it can be used to express a somewhat wicked delight that someone else has met with disappointment (sentence 1).

TALK A BLUE STREAK

to talk fast and at length

1. No one liked sitting at the lunch table with Phil because he had only one topic of conversation: his sports car. When it came to his car, Phil could *talk a blue streak*.

2. You can hardly get a word into a conversation with Wendy, the way she *talks a blue streak*.

Synonym: *talk (someone's) ear off; gift of gab*

TALK (SOMEONE'S) EAR OFF

to bore someone with one's unending talk

1. I try to keep my office door closed so that Jim won't come in. When he does, *he talks my ear off* and I can't get any work done.

2. Doug tried to signal me to interrupt his one-way conversation with Rita. It was obvious that she was *talking his ear off* and he was too polite to end the conversation.

Synonym: *bend (someone's) ear*

Compare to: *talk a blue streak*

Talk someone's ear off conveys a sense of boredom that may or may not be present in *talk a blue streak*.

TALK THROUGH (ONE'S) HAT

to speak without authority on some topic; to talk nonsense

1. Some people drink too much alcohol and then they begin to *talk through their hats*. They try to make you think that they know a lot about something when they really don't.

2. You should listen to Maria when she offers advice about buying real estate. She knows a lot about it. She's not just *talking through her hat*.

Compare to: *know beans about (something), not*

TALK TO (SOMEONE) LIKE A DUTCH UNCLE

person who talks to one like a close relative, giving advice that is sound, well-meant, and sometimes stern

1. The young man and woman were about to run away to get married, so the boy's brother took them aside and talked to them like a *Dutch uncle*. He told them that what they were doing was foolish.

2. The boy's father and mother could talk no sense into him, so they asked a teacher at the boy's school to *talk to him like a Dutch uncle*.

Similar to: *talk sense into (someone)*

TALK TURKEY

to talk seriously, usually about a business deal

1. I was ready to get serious about making an offer for the car. I was ready to *talk turkey*.

2. They were in agreement on their business deal; now all they had to do was work out the details. They sat down to *talk turkey*.

Compare to: get *down to business*

TALL ORDER
something difficult to accomplish

1. My boss wants me to finish all of this work by next Tuesday. It's a *tall order*—I'm going to have to work through the weekend.

2. My aunt is trying to cook dinner for our entire family without spending too much money. It's a *tall order*, but I think she can do it.

TAN (SOMEONE'S) HIDE/BRITCHES
to spank a child's bottom as punishment

1. Ricky didn't come home on time from his friend's house. When he got home, his mother *tanned his hide.*

2. That child is disrespectful and uncontrollable. What he really needs is for one of his parents to *tan his britches.*

The expression originates from the practice of tanning (preparing) animal hides (skins) for use as clothing or shoes by hitting them with a tanning instrument. *Hide* is also a slang word used to refer to a person's skin. The alternative *britches* (pants) refers to the fact that a person gets spanked on his bottom. The expression is usually used to describe how parents might punish their children.

THIRD-RATE
of poor quality

1. Let's get out of this *third-rate* hotel now. I know we can find a better one if we try.

2. The company fired Greg when the management decided that his work was *third-rate.*

Synonyms: *second-rate; fourth-rate*

Antonym: *first-rate*

The expression *third-rate* does not convey any ranked degree of inferiority when compared to second- or fourth-rate. All three expressions convey the same degree of inferiority.

THROUGH THICK AND THIN
in good times and bad times; steadfastly and loyally

1. My brother Tom has been there with me in good times and bad, through my joys and sorrows. He has always supported me *through thick and thin.*

2. No matter what happens to my husband, I'll stay with him *through thick and thin.* I'm sure he would do the same for me.

THROW DOWN THE GAUNTLET
to challenge someone to fight or argue

1. The candidate's opponent challenged her to debate the issues. The opponent had *thrown down the gauntlet* and she was ready to pick it up and accept the challenge.

2. If you don't want to start a fight with Carl, don't *throw down the gauntlet.*

A gauntlet is a glove from a suit of armor. The expression originates from a medieval custom of throwing down one's gauntlet as a way of challenging an enemy to a fight. One accepted the challenge by picking up the gauntlet.

THROW IN THE TOWEL
to stop trying; to quit

1. Roger had been trying hard to arrange a business deal between two groups. He was still unsuccessful after weeks of trying, so he decided to *throw in the towel* and spend his time on something else.

2. I'll never be able to pass my mathematics course, no matter how much time I spend studying. I'm going to *throw in the towel* and withdraw from the course.

The expression comes from the game of boxing. When a boxer has had enough and is ready to give up the fight, his or her manager throws the towel used to clean his or her face during the fight into the ring as a signal that the fight is over.

THROW THE BOOK AT (SOMEONE)
to give someone the harshest penalty or punishment allowed by law, or to impose any severe sentence or punishment

1. The judge decided to punish the thief to the full extent of the law. Instead of being lenient and giving him a light jail sentence, he *threw the book at him.*

2. The girl decided to buy the pack of gum instead of taking it without paying. She knew that if she got caught, they'd *throw the book at her.*

The *book* refers to a book of laws, and throwing it at someone means applying the maximum sentence a judge can legally impose upon a person convicted of a crime.

THROW/TOSS (ONE'S) HAT INTO THE RING
to announce one's candidacy for elected office

1. At first, Dan hadn't decided whether or not he wanted to run for governor, but now that he felt he had a good chance of winning, he was ready to *throw his hat into the ring.*

2. In order to get as much publicity for her campaign for mayor of the city as possible, Dr. Smith *tossed her hat into the ring* early.

Originates from 19th century boxing, during which men from the crowd would throw their hats into the boxing ring to indicate they wanted to challenge the latest winner.

TICKLE (SOMEONE'S) FANCY
to please or amuse someone in a light-hearted way

1. Fred decorated his garden with small animal statues because they *tickled his fancy.*

2. Before you decide that you don't want anything for your birthday, let's go to the jewelry store. You might see something there that *tickles your fancy.*

Compare to: *take a shine/fancy to (someone/ something); catch (someone's) fancy*

TICKLED PINK
thoroughly pleased; very happy

1. I'm just *tickled pink* that you'll be able to join us for dinner next Saturday. I'm really looking forward to it.
2. My niece got her first job today. She's so pleased with herself. She's *tickled pink*.

TIED TO (ONE'S) MOTHER'S APRON STRINGS
emotionally or physically attached to one's mother beyond what is considered appropriate and normal

1. Philip is 58 and still lives at home with his parents. He doesn't take care of himself. He still lets his mother take care of him. He's *tied to his mother's apron strings*.
2. Rachel decided to break off her engagement to Ted. She realized he would always take his mother's side in a dispute, and would always be *tied to his mother's apron strings*.

Compare to: *under (someone's) thumb*

An apron is a piece of clothing worn over the front of the body to protect normal clothing from getting dirty, especially when cooking. The apron is tied on with strings. The expression *tied to (one's) mother's apron strings* usually describes an adult's continued dependence on his or her mother.

TIE THE KNOT
to get married

1. Roger and Sue decided to get married. They are going to *tie the knot* in church on Saturday.
2. You don t need to rush into marriage. Why don't you give yourselves more time to think it over before you *tie the knot*?

The expression suggests that when two people get married, they tie a knot that binds them together.

TIGHTEN (ONE'S) BELT
to spend less money than one did previously

1. Marian lost her job so now the family has to make it on Sam's paycheck. They're going to have to *tighten their belts* and spend less until she finds another job.
2. My car broke down and I had to buy another one. Now I have less money for some of the things I used to be able to afford, so I've had to *tighten my belt*.

The expression suggests that a person loses weight because he or she is unable to buy as much food as he or she once did. As a result, he or she must tighten his belt so that his or her pants don't fall down.

TILT AT WINDMILLS
to fight against impossible odds in an attempt to do good

1. Don't waste your time and energy trying to change a situation that cannot be changed. The bureaucracy is too big to fight. You'll just be *tilting at windmills*.

2. I've always been one to try to help the helpless, even when I know I have little chance of success fighting against the powerful. I guess I'll always *tilt at windmills*.

The expression originates from Miguel de Cervantes's novel *Don Quixote*, in which Quixote comes upon several windmills and, thinking that they are giants, tries to defeat them in battle by tilting at them (stabbing while running or riding past) with his lance (long spear).

TIME ON (ONE'S) HANDS, HAVE (SOME)
to have free time with nothing to do

1. Can I help you fix a few things around the house today? I have some *time on my hands* until after dinner.
2. The children will get into trouble if they have too much *time on their hands*. We need to find something to keep them busy.

Synonym: *time to kill, have (some)*

The expression suggests a degree of boredom. Whereas *have time on one's hands* means only that one has some free time, *have time to kill* includes the notion that one is waiting for a future event.

TIME TO KILL, HAVE (SOME)
to have a period of time to pass while waiting for some future event

1. I expected the plane to leave at 4:30 but it has been delayed. Now I have some *time to kill* while I wait for the plane.
2. Sarah arrived at the meeting early. She had *time to kill* so she read a magazine.

Synonym: *time on (one's) hands*

The expression suggests that one must get rid of (kill) the extra time.

TIP OF THE ICEBERG, JUST/ONLY THE
the smallest, evident part of something that is much greater but hidden from view; more to a situation than one can see at the moment

1. This latest scandal in the government is only *the tip of the iceberg*. I'm convinced that there is much more corruption than what has been uncovered so far.
2. The police arrested the man they thought was guilty of the robbery. While they had him in jail, they began to uncover information that linked him to many of the robberies that had taken place over the last few years. This latest robbery was *just the tip of the iceberg*.

The expression suggests that while only the top of an iceberg may be visible, the larger and more dangerous portion of it is hidden from view under the water.

TIT FOR TAT
an action in exchange for another equal action

1. Mark criticized Pam's clothes and in return she criticized his haircut. It was *tit for tat*.

2. I didn't wash the dishes for you yesterday, and today you didn't take out the trash for me. I guess it's *tit for tat.*

Synonym: *give (someone) a taste of his own medicine; fix (someone's) wagon*

The expression may describe insults (sentence 1) or some harmless error (sentence 2).

TO BEAT THE BAND
in an exaggerated manner; with a lot of effort or to the extreme

1. The child was upset that she couldn't have any more candy. Her yelling and fussing was loud enough *to beat the band.*

2. The girl wanted to speak English better than anyone else. She decided she would have to practice *to beat the band* if she wanted to succeed.

The expression is used to describe physical activity. It is always used in the infinitive form but functions as an adverb.

TOE THE LINE
to follow the rules; to do what is expected of one

1. Mr. Kelly has survived in politics because he *toes the line.* He follows the policies of the majority and doesn't try to stand out or be different.

2. The boss didn't want any trouble from his workers. He told them they had better *toe the line* or get out.

Compare to: *straight and narrow*

The expression originates from an early form of boxing, in which a line was drawn on the ground and opponents had to keep the toes of one foot on the line during their fight. Any opponent who removed his toes from the line was disqualified from the fight.

TONGUE-IN-CHEEK
joking or sarcastic

1. When Paul complimented his secretary's work, he was being facetious. He meant just the opposite, but was *speaking tongue-in-cheek.*

2. Sometimes, the teacher seems like she's being serious, but she's really joking. What she says is *tongue-in-cheek.*

The expression describes a style of speech.

TOO BIG FOR (ONE'S) BRITCHES
to be sassy or arrogant, or to act or speak disrespectfully or inappropriately for one's age or position

1. Patty's mother scolded her, "Listen to me, young lady. You may not speak so rudely to anyone. You're getting *too big for your britches."*

2. His father told the little boy that his behavior was not acceptable in their house. He told the boy he was *too big for his britches* and he would be punished if he continued to misbehave.

The expression is usually used by parents to reprimand (scold) their children.

TOO MANY IRONS IN THE FIRE
too many activities demanding one's time

1. I have too many obligations on my time right now. I have *too many irons in the fire.*

2. Beth is going to exhaust herself with all the activities she has taken on. She has *too many irons in the fire.*

Synonym: *have (one's) hands full*

TOP OF THE LINE, THE
the best quality

1. I'd love to have a computer system that is *top of the line*, but I can't afford it right now so I'll have to settle for one that has fewer features.

2. The customer wanted to see every television model that the store had for sale. He wanted to see the lowest-priced standard model, as well as the model that was *top of the line.*

Antonym: *bottom of the barrel*

Compare to: *first-rate*

The line refers to a group of similar products or a group of products all manufactured by the same company.

TO THE HILT
to be fully committed to something; to do something completely

1. When my daughter thinks she's getting sick, she plays the role *to the hilt* so that she doesn't have to go to school. Even though she might just have a cold, she complains that she aches from head to toe.

2. They tried not to get into debt too much. But they had to get a bank loan to buy their house, so now they're in *to the hilt.*

Compare to: *go to town; pull out all the stops; whole hog; whole nine yards*

TOUCH AND GO
precarious or uncertain

1. I wasn't sure I'd get to the airport on time. First the taxi got stuck in a traffic jam and I was sure I wouldn't make it. Then the driver found a short cut and I was sure I would make it. Then we seemed to get all the red lights and again I was sure I wouldn't make it. It was *touch and go* the whole way.

2. The doctor told the woman her husband was out of danger now but that it had been *touch and go* the night before. The doctor hadn t been sure whether the man would live or die.

TRACK RECORD
a history of performance

1. The manager decided not to hire Steve because he had been fired from several of his previous jobs. He didn't have a very good *track record.*

2. The stockbroker recommended against investing in the company because it was fairly new and didn't have much of a *track record*. She suggested I consider the company again in a few years.

The expression originates from horse racing, in which a horse's previous wins and losses are studied in an effort to determine how well the horse will perform in the future.

TRAIN OF THOUGHT
a course of reasoning; a succession of connected ideas

1. Dianne couldn't seem to concentrate on her work. Her mind was wandering and she kept losing her *train of thought*.

2. The professor began writing mathematical calculations across the blackboard faster than anyone could follow her. The students couldn't follow her *train of thought*.

The expression suggests a series of thoughts connected together in some logical progression (not randomly), in the same way that the cars of a train are linked together one after another.

TREAT (SOMEONE) TO (SOMETHING)
to buy something for another person

1. Sarah was charmed when Chuck offered to *treat her to* an ice cream cone. She had expected to pay for it herself.

2. "Thanks for helping me with that project," said Ellie to her friend. "Let me *treat you to* lunch sometime."

This expression refers to buying something small and enjoyable for another person, such as a meal or some kind of small outing.

TROUBLED WATERS
emotionally rough times or an unsettled situation

1. I've noticed that you and your parents have been fighting a lot these days. I would like to help calm the *troubled waters* if I can.

2. Mr. Williamson has been someone that we could depend on for strength and comfort ever since our father died. He has been a bridge over *troubled waters*.

The expression uses the metaphor of rough (troubled) water and is frequently accompanied by related vocabulary such as "to calm or to pour oil on," "bridge over," "deep in," "wading into," etc.

TRUE BLUE
loyal and steadfast

1. I trust Marie completely. No one is more loyal than she is. She's *true blue*.

2. Silvia would change her allegiance without a second thought. She doesn't know the meaning of *true blue*.

TURN A DEAF EAR
to ignore someone

1. The child had been whining and crying all day. Eventually his mother *turned a deaf ear* and ignored him.

2. Grandfather has always been quarrelsome and difficult. He loves to complain to anyone who will listen. You just have to *turn a deaf ear* if you want to live in the same house with him.

Compare to: *fall on deaf ears*

TURNING POINT
a critical point

1. Michael's heart attack was a real *turning point* in his life. He changed his reckless ways and began eating better, exercising more, and relaxing more.

2. Anna had to decide whether she would pursue her career in dance or go into business. She realized that she could not do both. This decision would be a major *turning point* in her life.

Similar to: *make or break*

The expression suggests a fork in the road where one must turn in one direction or the other, depending on which path one chooses.

TURN OVER A NEW LEAF
to change one's bad ways and begin to lead a better life

1. The man promised the judge that he was finished with his life of crime and that he was ready to *turn over a new leaf*.

2. I know Phyllis says she's going to *turn over a new leaf*, but she continues to follow the same ways and befriend the same people.

Compare to: *wipe the slate clean*

The expression originates from the idea of life as a book full of pages (leaves). When one *turns over a new leaf*, one leaves behind a spoiled page of his or her life and turns to a fresh, clean page to start anew.

TURN (SOMETHING) THUMBS DOWN/UP {GIVE (SOMETHING) THE THUMBS DOWN/UP}
to vote yes or no to something

1. I presented my idea to the boss but he didn't like it at all. He *turned it thumbs down*.

2. They really liked the advertising campaign and gave it their whole-hearted approval. They *gave it the thumbs up*.

Synonym: *(thumbs down) nix something*

The expression originates from the Roman custom of turning a thumb downward to mean "no" or that something was unacceptable and upward to mean "yes" or that something was acceptable. People still use the thumbs-up or -down gesture, particularly when speaking or hearing is difficult.

TURN THE OTHER CHEEK

not to retaliate; not to pay back bad behavior with more bad behavior

1. When someone does something bad to you, you should not retaliate. Instead you should *turn the other cheek.*

2. Sometimes when people take advantage of me, it's difficult for me not to want to get back at them in revenge. It's hard to *turn the other cheek.*

Antonym: *pay (someone) back*

The expression originates from the New Testament of the Bible, in which Jesus teaches how one should respond to ill treatment.

TURN THE TABLES {THE TABLES HAVE TURNED}

to reverse a situation

1. Jane was poor when she started her own business and she struggled for a long time, but she finally *turned the tables* and now she's wealthy.

2. They were beating the other team in the first half, but *the tables have turned.* Now they're struggling to keep up and win the game.

Turn the tables originates from tabletop board games such as backgammon. During the game, players would turn the table (game) so they played from their opponent's position.

TURN UP (ONE'S) NOSE AT (SOMETHING/ SOMEONE)

to scorn, snub, or reject something

1. Mrs. Beasley wouldn't have anything to do with her new neighbors. She *turned up her nose at them* when they tried to make friendly conversation.

2. The child was so used to eating fresh vegetables that when I tried to feed him frozen vegetables, he *turned up his nose at them* and refused to eat.

Compare to: *give someone the cold shoulder*

Whereas *give someone the cold shoulder* is limited to people, *turn up one's nose* can be applied to people or things.

TURN UP THE HEAT

to apply or increase pressure to a person or situation

1. My parents have been nagging at me to get a job for several months, and now, they're *turning up the heat.* They've told me I'll have to move out if I don't get a job.

2. The lawyer *turned up the heat* and started to question the witness much more aggressively.

The expression suggests how pressure is created (or increased) when heat is applied to a pot of liquid on a stove.

U

UNDER A CLOUD

less than entirely trustworthy; suspected of some wrongdoing

1. The bank manager discovered that there was money missing from Mr. Jenkins' money drawer, and the manager suspected that Mr. Jenkins took it himself. Mr. Jenkins has been *under a cloud* ever since.

2. This administration has been marked by widespread corruption. Even if they manage to clean it up, the politicians will always be *under a cloud* of suspicion.

The lack of trust implied in the expression may or may not be justified.

UNDER (SOMEONE'S) THUMB

under someone's control

1. Don't ask Margie to make a change in our work schedule; she won't do anything without Larry's permission. She's *under Larry's thumb*.

2. Those two young people will never be allowed to make their own decisions or lead their own lives. Their mother will always control them. They will always be *under their mother's thumb*.

Compare to: *tied to (one's) mother's apron strings*

The expression suggests a dramatic difference between the person in control and the person who is controlled, the latter being so small or so weak as to be held down by a thumb.

UNDER THE TABLE/COUNTER

secretly or illegally

1. It is illegal for storekeepers to sell cigarettes or liquor to children, but some will sell them to children *under the counter*.

2. As a private investigator, I sometimes have to slip someone some money *under the table* in order to get information.

UNDER THE WEATHER

unwell; ill

1. John has not been looking very well these days. He's *under the weather*.

2. The children and I have had so many colds this winter. The whole family has been *under the weather* for weeks.

Antonym: *in the pink*

Whereas *in the pink* can be applied to people, animals, or machines, *under the weather* is applied only to people or animals.

UNDER THE WIRE

just in time before a deadline

1. The newspaper article was due no later than 4 o'clock and the editor got it in at exactly 3:59. He got it in right *under the wire*.

2. The deadline for applying to the university was the last day of March. Rachel procrastinated until it was almost too late, but then she stayed up all night filling out the application and got it in just *under the wire*.

Similar to: *in the nick of time; down to the wire*

UNTIL THE COWS COME HOME

until the end of the day; for a long time

1. When the young boy's mother refused to give him some candy, he started to cry. His mother told him he could cry *until the cows come home*, but he was not going to get any candy.

2. I will never be any good at giving speeches. I could practice *until the cows come home*, but I'll never get over being nervous when I have to stand up in front of a crowd.

The expression relates to herds of cows that graze outdoors during the day and then are brought inside for the night. It means "all day long."

UP IN ARMS

angry or upset

1. When the government raised the price of flour and sugar to the point where people could no longer afford them, the population was *up in arms*. Much of the population stopped work and gathered in the streets to protest.

2. The students were *up in arms* and began to protest against the school administration's policies. They marched on the administration building, carried signs calling for the president's resignation, and listened to speeches by the student leaders.

The expression is often used to describe groups of people rather than individuals. *Arms* refers to weapons. Thus the people are so angry that they are ready to take up weapons (at least figuratively).

UP IN THE AIR

unsettled or undecided

1. Jack wasn't sure whether to go to the university or get a job. His plans were *up in the air*.

2. I'm *up in the air* about remodeling my house or selling it and moving into a bigger one.

UPPER CRUST

the highest level of society, i.e. people who are separated from ordinary people as being elite either by economic or social position, or both

1. Queen Elizabeth and Prince Philip, and the other members of the English royal family, are members of high society. They are *upper crust*.

2. Only people with lots of money and the right social connections go to that university. It's a school for the *upper crust.*

The expression can be used either as an adjective (sentence 1) or as a noun (sentence 2*)*. Dating to the mid-19th century, this expression comes from the belief that the upper crust of bread was the best or most desirable part.

UPSET THE APPLE CART

to disturb the status quo; to shake up the existing situation

1. Everyone is happy with the situation as it is. If you try to change it, you'll be *upsetting the apple cart.*

2. The new president was installed and immediately *upset the apple cart* by appointing his own people to various positions in the administration.

Similar to: *rock the boat*

Whereas *rock the boat* usually describes a situation in which the people involved do not want a change, *upset the apple cart* can be used to describe any situation. The expression dates back to the Roman Empire and was originally 'upset the cart.' 'Apple' was added by the late 1700s.

UP THE CREEK (WITHOUT A PADDLE)

in a bad situation and unable to proceed; in an awkward position with no easy way out

1. Charles agreed to finish the report for his study group, but then discovered that the books he needed were only available in the library, and the library was closed. He was *up the creek.*

2. The city administrators expected to pay for street repairs from their existing budget but that money ran out when they had to pay for damages caused by unexpected storms. They were *up the creek without a paddle.*

Synonyms: *high and dry; leave (someone) in the lurch*

The expression suggests a situation where one is in a canoe on a small river without the means to navigate. It describes a situation in which one wants or needs to proceed but lacks the means.

UP TO SNUFF

meeting the minimum standard requirements; as good as is required

1. The orchestra didn t reach its usual high standard last year but with lots of extra practice this year, it's finally *up to snuff.*

2. I wasn't very happy with the last batch of dresses that came off the assembly line. The buttons fell off easily, the seams were not straight and the quality of the fabric was poor. The dresses really weren't *up to snuff.*

Synonym: *make the grade*

Compare to: *cut the mustard*

USE (ONE'S) WITS

to use one's intelligence, knowledge, or wisdom

1. Her problem is that she always reacts before considering what she should do first. She needs to learn to *use her wits* more.

2. *Use your wits*, boy! The answer is clear when you think about it.

WAIT FOR (ONE'S) SHIP TO COME IN
when one gets an unexpected lucky gift, especially money

1. Just give me a little more time to pay back the money I owe you. I don't have it right now, but I will *when my ship comes in*.
2. They keep saying that all their problems will be solved when they get rich. They're always *waiting for their ship to come in*, but it never will.

The expression probably originates from merchants who made their wealth when their goods came into port on a ship.

WALK IN (SOMEONE'S) SHOES
in someone else's situation

1. I wouldn't want to be *in your shoes* when your father finds out about the dent you put in his car.
2. It seems easy to tell others what to do or how to run their lives, but you can't really understand them until you have *walked in their shoes*.

WALKING ON AIR
blissfully happy

1. Lucy met Frank three weeks ago and fell madly in love with him. She's been *walking on air* ever since.
2. If Bruce gets accepted by Harvard Law School on a full scholarship, he will be *walking on air*.

Synonyms: *on cloud nine; seventh heaven*

The expression is always used in the present participle form. The past tense is formed by using "was/were" and the future tense is formed by using "will be."

WASH (ONE'S) HANDS OF (SOMETHING/SOMEONE)
to put something out of one's life or to stop claiming responsibility for something

1. I'm tired of trying to help my brother find a job, and I won't have anything further to do with him. I *wash my hands of the whole business*.
2. They agreed to go into business with their friend, but later found that he treated them unfairly. They decided they wanted nothing more to do with him, so they *washed their hands of him*.

WATER UNDER THE BRIDGE
past and finished; over and done with

1. John and I were married and divorced several years ago. I don't often think of him or wonder where he is now. That part of my life is *water under the bridge*.
2. Mary Ann had a bad experience when she was young, but she doesn't let herself think too much about it. It's *water under the bridge*.

The expression makes the analogy of life as a river of water. The water that has passed under the bridge is that part of a person's life that is past.

WAVE OF THE FUTURE, THE
a strong, growing trend

1. Wireless internet connections are the *wave of the future*. Soon, you won't need any cords at all.
2. It wasn't long ago that miniskirts were the *wave of the future*. Now they are a thing of the past.

WEAR (ONE'S) HEART ON (ONE'S) SLEEVE
to display one's feelings openly

1. Richard has never made a secret of his love for Jane. He has always *worn his heart on his sleeve*.
2. If you want to attract someone, sometimes you have to pretend you don t really care rather than *wearing your heart on your sleeve*.

The expression suggests that a person's heart (and therefore feelings) is exposed for all to see as though it were worn on the sleeve. In medieval Europe, knights used to tie to their sleeves handkerchiefs or ribbons representing the women they loved. In the 1700s, young men would wear the names of their sweethearts on their sleeves for Valentine's Day.

WEAR THE PANTS IN THE FAMILY
to make the major decisions and have the greatest amount of power in a family

1. Shelly and her husband disagreed on where to go on vacation, but they decided to work it out instead of fight. Neither one of them *wears the pants in the family*.
2. Who makes the decisions in your family? Who *wears the pants in your family*?

The expression suggests the stereotype of a traditional family in which the person who wears the pants (the man) is the person who controls the family.

WET BEHIND THE EARS
young and inexperienced

1. Ben is new to this business. He's *wet behind the ears*.
2. They haven't had much experience teaching yet. They're still *wet behind the ears*.

Antonym: *know the ropes*

Similar to: *born yesterday*

The expression comes from that fact that newly born (young) animals are wet at birth. Because of the close creases behind their ears, this area is usually the last to dry.

WET BLANKET
a person who is seen as never wanting to take part in fun activities; a person who ruins a good time

1. Don't invite Jerry to come along. He's a *wet blanket*, and he just ruins everyone's good time.

2. Why don't you relax and have a little fun? Don t be such a *wet blanket.*

This expression appears to come from the practice of using a wet blanket to put out campfires. If one thinks of the fire as being vibrant and exciting, then putting a *wet blanket* over it would extinguish or diminish that excitement.

WET (ONE'S) WHISTLE
to wet one's lips; to have a drink of something

1. After a hard day's work in the sun, I always enjoy *wetting my whistle* with a cold drink.

2. The singer needed to *wet his whistle* before he could continue singing.

WHAT IT'S CRACKED UP TO BE, (NOT)
not as good as its reputation; not as good as it is supposed to be

1. I thought this car was the best model around, but it's not *what it's cracked up to be.* Every week something else goes wrong with it.

2. You've traveled to the Caribbean islands. Are they everything you expected? Are they *what they're cracked up to be?*

The expression is used in the negative or question forms only.

WHEN HELL FREEZES OVER
never

1. My parents don't like me to drive alone. They'll buy me a car *when hell freezes over.*

2. Jake tried to get me to run a race with him, but I already know he's faster than I am. I'll race him *when hell freezes over.*

This expression indicates that something is so unlikely that it will only happen when a place as hot as hell freezes.

WHEN THE CHIPS ARE DOWN
when the situation is critical; when things are going badly

1. Henry is such a good friend. You can always count on him to help you *when the chips are down.*

2. Laura's a pleasant person, but she always seems to disappear when we need to get a project finished. *When the chips are down,* she's never around.

The expression probably originates from a game like poker in which the players use 'chips' to represent money they are betting. To be 'down on chips' would be to not have many, or much money, left.

WHIP/LICK (SOMEONE/SOMETHING) INTO SHAPE
to mold or assemble something into its proper shape quickly

1. The football coach told the players that they had been lazy all summer but that he was going to *lick them into shape* before the first game of the season.

2. We don't have much time left, and this report is due tomorrow. Do you think we have enough time to *whip it into shape?*

This expression comes from the very old belief that bear cubs were born misshapen and had to literally be *licked into shape* by their mothers and fathers. By the late 1600s, this phrase was being used with the figurative meaning it has now.

WHITE-COLLAR WORKER
an office worker

1. This company doesn t employ any manual laborers. Everyone who works for this company is a *white-collar worker.*

2. Dick likes to work outside in the fresh air and sunshine. He wouldn't be very happy as a *white-collar worker* in an office somewhere.

Antonym: *blue-collar worker*

The expression describes the color of the collar (and therefore the business shirt) worn by office workers. A manual laborer would not wear a white shirt because it would get dirty very quickly and be hard to keep clean.

WHITE ELEPHANT
an item that no one wants to buy or that is difficult to get rid of; a costly but useless possession

1. The salesman has been trying to get rid of that car for more than a year. It costs too much to run and insure, so no one wants it—it's a *white elephant.*

2. The department store is having a *white elephant* sale. They've reduced the prices on all the merchandise that they haven t been able to sell.

The item is usually not worthless, but for some reason other than cost, the item is difficult to sell. The origin of the expression is a traditional custom from Siam, present-day Thailand. If a rare albino (white) elephant was captured, it was the property of the emperor, and only he could ride or use the animal. Whenever the emperor wished to ruin someone who displeased him, he would give the man a white elephant. The man would then be forced to feed and care for the animal but could neither use nor destroy it.

WHITE LIE
a minor, polite, or harmless lie

1. When Jenny's parents asked her where she had gone, she told them she had been at the library, but she didn't tell them that she had also gone to the movies. She told her parents a *white lie.*

2. When Carol asked me what I thought of her new dress, I told her she looked good in it. I didn't really like the dress, but since I did not want to hurt Carol's feelings I told her a *little white lie.*

Similar to: *stretch the truth*

The expression suggests that a *white lie* is an innocent or inconsequential lie.

WHITEWASH

to conceal something bad; to make something look better than it really is

1. The boss doesn't want to get rid of his secretary, even though she has made some very costly mistakes. The boss simply keeps *whitewashing* the situation, pretending that her errors are insignificant.

2. The doctor told Susan's parents the truth about their daughter's condition. He felt it wouldn't be fair to *whitewash* the seriousness of Susan's illness.

The expression originates from the paint-like substance called whitewash, made from lime and water, which is used to paint houses and fences cheaply.

WHOLE KIT AND CABOODLE, THE

the entire amount; the whole lot

1. Some strangers came to our yard sale yesterday and bought everything we had. They bought *the whole kit and caboodle*.

2. When the landlord evicted the man, he cleared out all the man's possessions and put them out on the sidewalk, including the man's trash from his wastebaskets! He put out *the whole kit and caboodle*.

Synonym: *lock, stock, and barrel*

The expression is often used to describe items which might not normally be included or which one might expect to be excluded, such as the trash from the wastebaskets (sentence 2). Dating from the late 1800s, *the whole kit and caboodle* is actually the combination of words with a similar meaning. Both *kit* and *caboodle* mean a collection, and the combination into a single phrase is a way of adding emphasis.

WHOLE NINE YARDS, GO THE

the entire amount; (to go) all out

1. The girl's father decided to spare no expense in getting the very best of everything for his daughter's wedding. He *wanted the whole nine yards*.

2. We could save a little money on this dress by using less cloth in the skirt if you don't want to *go the whole nine yards*.

Compare to: *pull out all the stops; go to town; go whole hog*

The term comes from the World War II era where a fighter pilot's chain of ammunition was twenty-seven feet long (or nine yards). So when he fired all this on the target, he said "I gave it the whole nine yards" — meaning, he gave it all he had.

WILD-GOOSE CHASE

a useless or difficult search

1. First my cousin told me I could buy what I needed at one store; then she sent me to three more. I never did find it. She sent me on *a wild-goose chase*.

2. Tom went all over town from one office to another trying to find out how he could apply to change his citizenship. At the end of the day, he was no closer to finding out, and he had been on *a wild-goose chase*.

This expression is first recorded in Shakespeare's play *Romeo and Juliet*, and at that time actually referred to horse racing, not birds as the as the phrase might imply. In horse racing a *wild-goose chase* was a type of racing where the horses run in a V-like formation, similar to the way birds fly. Later, the connection to horse racing was lost in use, and people assumed the phrase came from flying geese.

WING IT

to improvise; to do something without planning or preparation

1. Today is the day I'm supposed to present my report to the board of directors, but I'm not at all prepared. When I stand up in front of them, I'm going to have to *wing it*.

2. We don't know how we're going to handle the situation. It's hard to plan for something like this in advance, so we'll just *wing it* and hope for the best.

Similar: *by the seat of (one's) pants*, *play it by ear*

Dating from the late 19th century, *wing it* was originally a theatrical term. Impromptu (unprepared) actors would quickly look over their speaking lines before going onto stage and then someone in the wings (behind the stage curtains) would prompt the actors on their exact lines.

WIPE THE SLATE CLEAN

to set a situation right or erase something bad

1. I know I'm in trouble for misbehaving in class last week, but I want to do better. I want to *wipe the slate clean*.

2. When Kyle was rude to his mother, she sent him to his room, but his punishment was over by dinner time. The *slate had been wiped clean*.

A *slate* is a small chalkboard.

WITH BATED BREATH

hardly breathing at all because of fear, excitement, or other strong emotion

1. Alan took out a small ring. Jennifer knew this was the moment, and she waited *with bated breath* for him to ask her to marry him.

2. The swimmer stood silently *with bated breath* as he waited for the starter's gun to go off.

Bated is a shortened form of *abated*, which means to lessen or put on hold. The first recorded use of *bated* is in 1596 in Shakespeare's play *Merchant of Venice*: "With bated breath, and whisp'ring humblenesse." The expression is used in situations in which someone is waiting tensely for something to happen.

WITH FLYING COLORS

triumphantly; victoriously

1. We weren't sure how the boys would do on their exams, but they passed *with flying colors*.

2. You look so nervous, but I know you can do it. Don't worry; you'll sail through *with flying colors*.

Large ships often sailed into ports with their flags (colors) raised and flying in the wind. This image of glory and victory was eventually extended to any event through which one became triumphant.

WOLF IN SHEEP'S CLOTHING

someone who presents himself as a harmless person, but who has intentions that are not honorable

1. The police have been looking for that criminal for months. He approaches people and pretends he is selling them valuable stocks that are really worthless. He's a *wolf in sheep's clothing*.

2. John is such a good-looking young man, women are attracted to him quickly. It's easy to see why people who don't know him think he is probably a *wolf in sheep's clothing*, when he is really a gentleman.

The expression comes from Aesop's fable of the wolf that, in order to get close to a flock of sheep it wants to eat, clothes itself in a sheepskin to avoid detection.

WRONG SIDE OF THE TRACKS, COME FROM THE

the poor part of town

1. Sharon knew her parents would never approve of her marriage to Ricky because he *came from the wrong side of the tracks*.

2. Mr. and Mrs. Dawson didn t want their children to attend Smithson High School because it was on the *wrong side of the tracks* and it might be dangerous for the children to walk from home to school by themselves.

The expression suggests that towns or cities are divided into a right (i.e. rich) side and a wrong (i.e. poor) side by the railroad tracks that run through them. The expression is often used to describe where someone comes from.

YELLOW {HAVE A YELLOW STREAK}
cowardly

1. Peter isn't brave enough to stand up and fight. He's *yellow.*

2. I bought this big dog for protection from burglars, but he's a coward. He has a *yellow streak* a mile long.

YELLOW JOURNALISM
journalism that is exaggerated or unnecessarily sensational

1. Some of the newspapers that are for sale at the checkout counter of the supermarket have headlines that are sensational as well as untrue. They are an example of *yellow journalism.*

2. Some newspaper reporters resort to *yellow journalism* to sell more copies of their newspapers. They unnecessarily report the shocking details of events such as murders just to get headlines that catch the eye.

Part 2
Selected Idioms by Category

In this part, selected idioms are organized into categories. The idioms were chosen because they are commonly used and understood by native English speakers in the United States. These lists are not meant to be complete; many more idioms could be added to these categories. In addition, some of the idioms below could be put into more than one category. Teachers might use these categories for organizing exercises or focusing discussions. There are sample questions using these categories on pages 105-118.

People

DESCRIPTIONS OF PEOPLE (NOUNS)
Apple of one's eye
Big shot
Big fish in a small pond
Big wheel
Bigwig
Blue-blood
Blue-collar worker
Bull in a china shop
Chip off the old block
Eager beaver
Fish out of water
Good egg
Head honcho
Heavyweight
Jack of all trades
Lame duck
Low man on the totem pole
Old fuddy-duddy
Salt of the earth
Stuffed shirt
White-collar worker

ABOUT PEOPLE (ADJECTIVES)
All wet
Filthy rich
First-rate
Footloose and fancy free
Green around the gills
Keyed up
Knee-high to a grasshopper
Too big for one's britches
Up to snuff
Upper crust
Wet behind the ears

Conversation

All kidding aside
Beat around the bush
Bend someone's ear
Butt in
Butter someone up
Clam up
Clear the air
Clown around
Get a word in edgewise

Gift of gab
Give someone a ring
Give someone a song and dance
Heart to heart
Hit the nail on the head
Hold one's tongue
Lend someone an ear
Make a long story short
Make a mountain out of a molehill
On the tip of one's tongue
Pass the buck
Pick someone's brain
Pull rank
Pull strings
Pull the rug out from under someone
Pull the wool over someone's eyes
Put someone on the spot
Say a mouthful
See eye to eye
Shoot the breeze
Spill the beans
Spring something on someone
Stand one's ground
Stick one's nose in
Straight from the horse's mouth
Stretch the truth
String someone along
Talk a blue streak
Talk turkey
Turn a deaf ear
Wing it

Emotions/Feelings

SUCCESS AND HAPPINESS
Blue-blood
Blue ribbon
Carry a torch for someone
Charmed life, lead a
Cream of the crop
Dressed to kill
Footloose and fancy-free
Go to town
Gravy train
Happy-go-lucky
Have/got it made
Head over heels in love
In the chips/money
In the pink
Keep up with the Joneses
Lap of luxury, live in the
Life of Riley
Midas touch
On cloud nine

Pop the question
Roll out the red carpet
Seventh heaven, in
Sitting pretty
Strike it rich
Sweep someone off his/her feet
Through thick and thin
Tickle someone's fancy
Tickled pink
Tie the knot
Top of the line, the
Upper crust
With flying colors

ANGER/BEING UPSET
At the end of one's rope
At loggerheads
Ax to grind
Blow off steam
Boiling point
Chew someone out
Fly off the handle
Get up on the wrong side of the bed
Get someone's dander/hackles up
Give someone a hard time
Give someone a piece of one's mind
Give someone a taste of his own medicine
Go bananas
Hopping mad
Hot under the collar
Lose one's cool
On the warpath
Put one's foot down
Put the squeeze/screws on/to
Speak one's mind

ILL HEALTH
Black and blue
Blue
Burned out
Down and out
Fall off the wagon
Go to pot
Go to seed
Go to the dogs
Know if one is coming or going, not
Look/feel like death warmed over
Off one's rocker
On one's last legs
Under the weather

NEGATIVE SITUATIONS
In a bind
In a jam
In a rut

In Dutch
In hot water
In over one's head
In the doghouse

Time

At the drop of a hat
Burn the midnight oil
Days are numbered, (someone's/something's)
Down to the wire
Eleventh hour
From the word go
In the long run
In the nick of time
Jump the gun
Mark time
On hold, put something
On ice, put something
Once in a blue moon
Shake a leg
Slow/quick off the mark
Spur of the moment, on the
Step on it
Time on one's hands, have some
Time to kill, have some
Under the wire
Until the cows come home

Money

Black market
Bottom line, the
Bring home the bacon
Buy (something) for a song
Cost (someone) a mint/an arm and a leg
Cut corners
Drop in the bucket
Dutch treat (Go Dutch)
Feather one's nest
Feel the pinch
Flat broke
Go broke
Hit pay dirt
Hit the jackpot
In the black
In the chips/money
In the red
Make ends meet
Midas touch
Money to burn
Pay through the nose
Penny pincher

Pinch pennies
Put one's money where one's mouth is
Sales pitch
Save (something) for a rainy day
Sell like hotcakes
Strike it rich
Take someone to the cleaners
Tighten one's belt
Wait for one's ship to come in

Job/Work

Back to the drawing board
Burn the candle at both ends
Get down to business
Keep one's nose to the grindstone
Old-boy network
Pencil/paper pusher
Pink slip
Pull rank
Rank and file

Part 3

Classroom Activities

Idioms are an integral part of the English language. They are used often by almost all native speakers of English. Some are used often by some people, but not by others. There are some that everyone understands, but hardly anybody uses. Some are used and understood in some parts of the English-speaking world and not in others. Because idioms are rooted so strongly in culture and used in very specific situations, it is difficult for English language learners to know what idioms are used in what situations and by whom. That's a *tall order*! (A tall order is a very difficult and complex task.)

The best way to begin a study of idioms is to improve comprehension. We suggest that the teacher first focus on understanding definitions and situations so that students can make sense of what they hear or read.

The following classroom activities begin with tasks that focus on comprehension and progress to tasks that require speaking. Many of the activities in Part Three refer to the categories of idioms listed in Part Two. We encourage teachers to use their imaginations in creating integrated activities around idioms. The suggestions here are only a *jumping-off point*. (A jumping-off point is a starting place to help ideas develop.)

And remember, idioms are **fun!** You don't need to learn them all to speak English well, but knowing just a few can help make your English more colorful.

Matching

Purpose/Goal: to recognize idiom meanings

Number of Participants: any number

Materials: teacher-made handout with idioms and definitions

Procedure

1. Select up to ten idioms from this book.

2. Write the idioms on the left side of the paper (or board) and the definitions on the right side.

3. Ask students to write the letter of each definition next to the corresponding idiom.

Sample

1. _____ Eleventh hour   **a.** unusual

2. _____ Keyed up   **b.** anxious

3. _____ Off the wall   **c.** late

4. _____ Take off   **d.** inexperienced

5. _____ Wet behind the ears   **e.** move quickly

Multiple Choice

Purpose/Goal: to recognize appropriate idioms in context

Number of Participants: any number

Materials: teacher-made handout with sentences and idioms

Procedure

1. Select idioms from this book.

2. Write a sentence using each idiom, but leave a blank space for the idiom.

3. Give students three or four idioms that might belong in the blank, and ask them to choose the correct one.

Sample

1. Our company has been (<u>losing money</u>) for over three years now.
   a. in the pink
   b. in the red
   c. in the black
   d. in black and white

2. My father can do anything; he's a _____.
   a. Jack of all trades
   b. fish out of water
   c. bull in a china shop
   d. lame duck

Memory *(Card Game 1)*

Purpose/Goal: to recognize meanings

Number of Players: 2 – 10

Materials: teacher-made cards (30) marked with idioms and definitions

Procedure

1. Choose 15 idioms that you want your students to learn. Write each one down on a card or slip of paper.

2. On 15 more cards, write the definitions to the idioms.

3. Mix the cards up and place them face-down on a table.

4. Taking turns, the students turn two cards over to show the writing. Is there an idiom and a definition? Do they match? If they match, the student keeps the cards. If not, the student turns them back over and the next person takes a turn.

5. The student with the most matches at the end of the game is the winner.

Variation

Instead of writing the idioms and definitions on cards, write them on the blackboard in random order. Before the students are in the room, tape a piece of paper over each word and each definition. Play the game by having students come up one at a time to the board and remove two pieces of paper to see if they match. If they match, erase the words. If they don't match, replace the papers to cover the words and choose another student to come to the board.

Sorting *(Card Game 2)*

Purpose/Goal: to identify similarities

Number of Players: 1– 6 in each group

Materials: teacher-made cards (30 per group) marked with idioms

Procedure

1. Select about 30 idioms and write them on cards or slips of paper.

2. Write the same set of idioms for each group of five or six students.

3. Ask students to sort the idioms into categories by meaning.

4. Students can check this book or another source for the meanings, if necessary.

Variation 1 (Easiest)

Give students categories and tell them how many words are in each category. For example, 'The categories are idioms about happiness, anger, sadness, and ill health. There are six in each category.'

Variation 2 (Harder)

Don't give students any categories. Let them develop their own. Follow up by asking students to write their categories on the board. For example, 'I'm not going to tell you the topics of the categories. Try to figure them out yourselves. You may come up with your own categories.'

Idiom-a-week

Purpose/Goal: to notice selected idioms

Number of Participants: any number

Materials: none

Procedure

1. Choose an idiom to be the idiom of the week.

2. Post the idiom somewhere in your classroom for all students to see—for example, at the top of your blackboard.

3. Students must find the meaning of the idiom in this book, in their dictionaries, on the internet, or in other resources.

4. Ask students to compare their findings with each other to see how many different ways the idiom is used.

5. Have students keep track of how many times they hear or read that idiom during the week.

Pocket Reminders

Purpose/Goal: to use all five senses to learn idioms

Number of Participants: any number

Materials: small blank cards or slips of paper

Procedure:

1. Have each student choose an idiom from this book or another source.

2. Have each student write the idiom on a slip of paper or index card.

3. Ask each student to put the idiom in his or her pocket and keep it there for the whole week. Each time they see or touch the slips of paper, they will be reminded of their idioms. They can also try to use the idiom in their English language conversations during the week.

Note to Teacher

This idea is based on the theories of peripheral learning. If students are surrounded by new vocabulary and take it in through all of their senses, they will have a better chance of learning and remembering words or phrases. The pocket reminder uses the sense of touch as a learning tool.

Idiom Journal

Purpose/Goal: to keep active, individualized lists

Number of Participants: any number

Materials: journal paper or writing books

Procedure:

Have each student keep an idiom journal. This is a list of idioms they have used, either in speech or writing. (If students are already keeping a vocabulary journal, have them designate a separate section just for idioms.)

Variation 1

Students can write down the idioms that they plan to use in the next week. They then can check them off once they have used them.

Variation 2

Students can keep track of how many times they have used a new idiom, either spoken or written.

Variation 3

Students can use their journal to write down new idioms they discover. These new vocabulary items may come from movies, books, magazines, or television. They can share and compare these with their classmates and then find their meanings in their resource books or on the internet.

Note to Teacher

An idiom journal is not just a list of phrases; it should be an interactive tool for learning. If students are actively engaged in their learning, they have a better chance of retaining learned material. By writing their own journals, students strengthen their own learning strategies and improve their opportunities for acquisition.

Comparison of Expressions

Purpose/Goal: to compare idioms or expressions in two languages

Number of Participants: any number

Materials: none

Procedure:

1. Prepare a list of English idioms that have meanings similar to idioms or expressions in the students' L1.

2. Variation: Ask students to think of an expression in their own language that has a meaning similar to an English idiom.

3. Ask students to write the phrase in their L1 and to translate it into English.

4. Discuss and compare the similarities and differences between the two languages.

Sample

	English	Your Language
1.	Head over heels in love	_____
2.	Under the weather	_____
3.	In hot water	_____
4.	Shoot the breeze	_____
5.	Beat around the bush	_____

Write an Idiom Story

Purpose/Goal: to use idioms in personal stories

Number of Participants: any number

Materials: paper

Procedure:

1. Have students think of an especially eventful day in their lives.

2. Tell them to turn to a partner and tell him/her about that day.

3. After both partners have talked, give students 20 to 30 minutes to write a narrative of the day's events: who they met, how they felt, what they did. (This can also be done as homework.)

4. Have students read their own writing again, and add appropriate idioms to their stories.

5. Ask the students to exchange papers and read their partners' narratives. Have students suggest idioms that their partners might use, explaining why they think each idiom is appropriate.

6. Have each student tell the rest of the class what idioms they have used in their writing.

Note to Teacher

Contextualizing idioms is very difficult. Idioms are so deeply connected to cultural identity and communication norms that non-native speakers have difficulty in using them correctly. This activity is for advanced speakers of English. It is not meant to be an activity with right and wrong answers. It is meant to give learners a chance to 'play' with idioms in the context of their own writing.

Discussion Questions

Purpose/Goal: to reinforce comprehension of selected idioms

Number of Participants: any number

Materials: none

Procedure:

> The following discussion questions are based on idioms in the categories in Part Two of this book. After teaching the selected idioms, use the following example questions as whole-class or small-group discussions. These are open-ended follow-up discussions that reinforce the meanings of idioms.

Category: People *(page 101)*

1. Describe the members of your family or a group you belong to.

   Who is a *chip off the old block?* In what ways is he or she? How is he or she not?

   Who is the *apple of your father's eye?* Is it you or one of your brothers or sisters?

   Who is *a big shot* / an *eager beaver* / a *good egg?*

2. What happened to your grandmother (grandfather/mother/aunt/etc.) when she was *knee high to a grasshopper?*

3. Discuss the characteristics of someone you know who is the *salt of the earth.*

4. Describe someone you know who is a *stuffed shirt.*

5. What work would someone do if he were a *white-collar worker /* a *blue-collar worker?*

6. Who would you rather marry, a *good egg* or a *Jack of all trades?* Why?

7. Would you rather be *footloose and fancy free* or *filthy rich?* Why?

8. Do you know anyone who is an *old fuddy duddy?* Who?

Category: Conversation *(page 101-102)*

1. Tell us about people who don't let you *get a word in edgewise*.

2. Talk about a time when you had a *heart to heart* talk with a parent.

3. Do you know someone who *sticks his/her nose in* other people's business? What does he or she do?

4. Discuss a time when a teacher put you *on the spot*.

5. Tell us about somebody you like to *shoot the breeze* with.

6. Talk to your friends about a time when you *got something off your chest*.

7. When should you *lend someone an ear?*

8. Name a topic that you *don't know beans about*.

Category: Success and Happiness *(page 102)*

1. What makes you feel *tickled pink?*

2. Have you ever felt like you were *on cloud nine?* Tell your friends about it.

3. When have you felt *happy-go-lucky?* What made you feel that way?

4. Do you know someone who leads *a charmed life?* In what ways?

5. Have you ever felt *head over heels in love?* What did you do?

6. What is the best thing to say to *pop the question?*

7. What would a woman wear if she is *dressed to kill?* What would a man wear?

8. Does your family *keep up with the Joneses?* How?

Category: Anger/Being Upset *(page 102)*

1. When was the last time you *flew off the handle?* What did you do?

2. Have you ever *lost your cool or gone bananas?* How did other people react?

3. What makes you *hopping mad?*

4. When were you *at the end of your rope?* How did you help yourself feel better?

5. Talk about a time when someone was *on the warpath/rampage*.

6. What might happen to make you *chew someone out?*

7. Did you *get up on the wrong side of the bed* this morning? Or any other morning?

8. Did your mother or father ever *put his or her foot down* when you wanted to do something? What?

Category: Ill Health *(page 102)*

1. What makes you feel better when you are *under the weather?*

2. When was the last time that you were *black and blue?* What happened?

3. What makes you feel *burned out?*

4. Have you every felt *down and out?* What was the situation?

5. Have you ever felt like just letting yourself *go to pot?* When? Why?

6. Tell you friends about a time when you *didn't know if you were coming or going*.

7. How would you describe someone who is *off their rocker?*

8. How do you cheer yourself up when you are *blue?*

Category: Negative Situations *(page 102-103)*

1. Have you ever been in a situation where you felt you were *in over your head*? Tell your friends about it.

2. Have you ever been *in a jam*? What got you there? What got you out?

3. Tell your friends about a time when you were *in hot water* with your teacher/boss.

4. If you are *in a rut*, what do you do to get yourself out of it? What about your friends?

5. When you were a kid, were you ever *in the doghouse*? How did your parents punish you?

6. If a friend comes to you and says, 'I am *in a bind*,' what do you do?

Category: Time *(page 103)*

1. Discuss something you do *once in a blue moon*.

2. Tell your classmates about a party where you danced *till the cows came home*.

3. When you have *time to kill?* What do you do?

4. Is there something you would do *at the drop of a hat?*

5. Tell us about times when you had to *burn the midnight oil*.

6. What have you done *in the nick of time?*

7. What have you done on the *spur of the moment?*

8. If you have *time to kill* today, what will you do?

Category: Money *(page 103)*

1. Who *brings home the bacon* in your family?

2. Tell us about something that *cost your family a mint*.

3. What you would do with *money to burn?*

4. Talk about something you *bought for a song*.

5. Do you know a *penny pincher?* What do they do?

6. Have you ever been *flat broke?* What did you do?

7. How much money should you *save for a rainy day?*

8. Is it ever appropriate to *go Dutch* in your country? With whom and in what situation?

Index

Idioms Referenced by Page Numbers

F

Face the music 7, 24, 38, 89
Fair and square 24, 83
Fair shake, get/give (someone) a 24
Fair to middling 24
Fair-weather friend 24
Fall by the wayside 24
Fall for (someone) 24, 43, 71
Fall for (something) 24
Fall off the wagon 24, 104
Fall on deaf ears 25, 93
Far cry from (something) 25
Fat cat 25
Feather in (one's) cap vi, 25, 60, 82
Feather (one's) nest 25, 105
Feel (something) in (one's) bones [have a feeling in (one's) bones] 25
Feel the pinch 25, 86, 105
Field day 25
Fight tooth and nail 25
Fill/fit the bill 25, 42
Filthy rich 26, 35, 103, 117, 120
Fine kettle of fish 26
Fine-tooth comb 26
First-rate 17, 26, 28, 79, 90, 92, 103
Fish out of water 26, 46, 66, 103, 109
Fishy 26
Fits and starts 26
Fix (someone's) wagon 26, 35, 91, 92
Flash in the pan 26
Flat broke 26, 35, 105, 117, 120
Fly-by-night 27
Fly in the face of (something) 27
Fly in the ointment 27
Fly off the handle 8, 27, 49, 56, 74, 79, 104, 118
Fly the coop 27
Follow in (someone's) footsteps 15, 27, 83, 117
Food for thought 14, 27
Fool around 16, 27, 43, 59
Fool's gold 27
Footloose and fancy-free 28, 103, 104, 117
Forbidden fruit 28
Force to be reckoned with, a 28
For crying out loud 28, 37
For goodness' sake 28, 37
For heaven's sake 28, 37
For the birds 2, 4, 5, 22, 28, 51, 62, 64, 67, 79
Forty winks 28
Fourth-rate 17, 26, 28, 79, 90, 92
From day one 29
From the word go 29, 105
Full steam ahead 29

G

Get a handle on (something) 30
Get (a) hold of (oneself) 30, 36
Get (a) hold of (someone) 30
Get (a) hold of (something) 30
Get a leg up 30

Get a move on 30, 80
Get a word in edgewise 30, 103, 118
Get by 30, 49, 57
Get caught/be left holding the bag [leave (someone) holding the bag] 30, 54, 96
Get down to brass tacks/business/the nitty gritty 31, 32, 60, 89, 105
Get/give (someone/something) short shrift 33
Get/give (someone) the cold shoulder 33
Get/give (someone) the go-ahead 32, 33
Get/give (someone) the green light 33
Get/give (someone) the sack 33, 70
Get/give (someone) the short end of the stick 33
Get/give (someone) the third degree 33
Get/give the go-ahead 32, 33
Get/have (something) down pat 33
Get/hit (something) on the nose 32
Get it in the neck 31
Get/lend (someone) a hand 34
Get off/go scot-free 31
Get off (one's) high horse 31
Get (one's) act/it together 30, 31, 51, 64, 67
Get (one's) second wind 31
Get (someone's) dander/hackles up 10, 31, 76, 80, 104
Get (something) off (one's) chest 32, 118
Get (something) through (one's) head 32
Get the message 32
Get this show on the road 31, 32, 89
Get to the bottom of (something) 32
Get to the point 5, 32, 41, 85
Get-up-and-go 32
Get up on the wrong side of the bed 33, 104, 119
Gift of gab, the 34, 89, 104
Give in 24, 34, 51, 83, 84, 85
Give (one's) right (body part) for/to do (something) 34
Give (someone) a hard time 34, 104
Give (someone) a piece of (one's) mind 13, 14, 34, 72, 74, 82, 104
Give (someone) a ring 34, 104
Give (someone) a snow job 16, 34, 71, 78, 104
Give (someone) a/some song and dance 16, 34, 71, 78, 104
Give (someone) a taste of (his/her) own medicine 26, 35, 91, 92, 104
Give (someone/something) a wide berth 35
Give (someone) the cold shoulder 35
Give (someone) the shirt off (one's) back 35
Go against the grain 35
Go around in circles 35
Go bananas [drive (someone) bananas] 2, 3, 15, 35, 36, 49, 104, 118
Go broke 26, 35, 105, 120
Go for broke 35
Go haywire 2, 3, 15, 30, 35, 36, 49
Go it alone 36
Golden age 37
Good egg 37, 103, 117
Good grief 28, 37
Good samaritan 38
Go off half-cocked 36, 78
Go off the deep end 36
Go out on a limb 36, 85
Go overboard 36

W

Y